Visions of God

Visions of GOD

Four Medieval Mystics and Their Writings

KAREN ARMSTRONG

BANTAM BOOKS

New York   Toronto   London
Sydney   Auckland

VISIONS OF GOD

A Bantam Book/December 1994

Library of Congress Cataloging-in-Publication Data

Armstrong, Karen.
  Visions of God : four medieval mystics and their writings /
Karen Armstrong.
    p.   cm.
  Includes bibliographical references.
  Contents: Richard Rolle of Hampole — Author of The cloud of
unknowing — Walter Hilton — Dame Julian of Norwich.
  ISBN 0-553-35199-0
  1. Mysticism — England — History.   2. Mysticism — History —
Middle Ages, 600-1500. I. Title
  BV5077.E54A76   1994
  248.2'2'092242-dc20   94-20217
                                                            CIP

Published simultaneously in the United States and Canada

Bantam Books are published by Bantam Books, a division of Bantam
Doubleday Dell Publishing Group, Inc. Its trademark, consisting of the
words "Bantam Books" and the portrayal of a rooster, is Registered in U.S.
Patent and Trademark Office and in other countries. Marca Registrada.
Bantam Books, 1540 Broadway, New York, New York 10036.

PRINTED IN THE UNITED STATES OF AMERICA
FFG   0 9 8 7 6 5 4 3 2 1

Contents

Introduction

Until recently, each of the great religions of the world developed independently and had little contact with one another. In each of the far-flung corners of the civilized world, men and women pondered the flawed and tragic conditions of human life and attempted to find a solution that would enable them to survive the suffering that flesh is heir to. In the period of transition that historians call the Axial Age (800–200 B.C.E.), the great confessional faiths developed that have continued to be a crucial influence in the consciousness of the people of each region: In China, Lao Tsu developed Taoism; in India, Hinduism and Buddhism re-formed the primitive pagan vision and made it a means of analyzing the self; in the Middle East, the monotheistic faiths analyzed history and the Greek rationalists of Athens analyzed the cosmos to find an ultimate meaning and significance in the apparently random flux of life. For geographical and political reasons, there was little contact between the various religious systems. In the Middle East there was a tradition of religious pluralism and the new faiths of Judaism and Zoroastrianism and — later — Christianity and Islam coexisted in relative harmony; in India during the seventeenth century, some Muslims and Hindus pooled their ideas and attempted to find a common vision: Sikhism was born of this attempt. But in general the world religions kept to themselves, separated by linguistic, cultural, and geographical barriers that seemed insuperable. Each religion developed its own particular insight, but had to cater to a number of different needs: If you were born in India, for example, you were likely to be either a Buddhist or a Hindu. It was not possible to seek an alternative faith in China or Greece. Men and women, therefore, had to work out their salvation in a particular religious perspective and the original faith had to be adapted to meet the inclinations and spiritual gifts of all its members.

In the twentieth century, however, there has been a major change. The improved communications are beginning to enable ordinary men and women to understand and appreciate systems of faith and belief that would once have seemed impossibly alien. For the first time in history, people are beginning to adopt the religion of other cultures or are finding inspiration in more than one faith. Thus, Buddhism is enjoying a great flowering in the West at present; Jesuit priests are studying meditation from Zen practitioners; Christians have been profoundly influenced by the thought and spirituality of the Jewish philosopher and theologian Martin Buber; and the great classics of religious literature have been ably translated and are easily accessible. The effect of this change could be profound: It has been compared to the revolution that science produced in the consciousness of men and women during the nineteenth and early twentieth centuries. We shall never be able to look at either our own or other people's religions in quite the same way again.

One of the lessons we have already begun to learn is the almost uncanny universality of the religious experience. Men and women may express their faith in different terms, but there is an underlying and profound similarity beneath all the

differences. We now realize that the great religions of the
world are not monolithic institutions but that they all contain
several spiritualities — many of which are found right across
the board of the world religions — which reflect different attitudes of mind toward our ultimate end. Mysticism is one such
spirituality found in all religions, and it is a startling example
of this deep unity of the religious vision. Mystics often have
different beliefs, and these inevitably affect their experience;
they will describe their interior journeys in terms of the orthodox traditions of their faith. Jews, Christians, and Muslims,
for example, believe in a personal God, while Buddhists feel
that this is an unreligious idea and prefer to speak of an
ultimate but indescribable Reality. But the actual experience
of all mystics is strikingly similar: All encounter a reality in the
depths of the self that is, paradoxically, Other and irrevocably
separate from us. All emphasize that this ultimate reality,
which gives meaning and value to human life, is ineffable,
transcending our limited words and concepts. Mystics are
aware that their experience can never be explained in rational
terms and insist that it is unhelpful and can even be dangerous
to attempt to define the ultimate reality in terms of reason and
logic. They encounter a presence that transfigures their lives
and, provided that they are temperamentally suited to this
type of spiritual activity and have the benefit of expert advice,
they experience a satisfaction that is real but inexpressible.
They feel that they have transcended the confines of their
limited and isolated egos and also feel that they have been
somehow absorbed into the ultimate truth and are at one with
the world.

People who have no religious faith find this baffling, but
it would be wrong to dismiss the mystic as deluded and
credulous. However one chooses to interpret it, the mystical
experience has been a fact of life ever since human consciousness had developed to a particular point. Mysticism is not for

everybody, however. Certain men and women have a propensity for this type of spirituality and have devised techniques and disciplines to create this sense of presence within themselves. Again, these techniques are revealingly similar in widely different cultural contexts. At the very least, therefore, mysticism must tell us something important about the human mind. Buddhists, indeed, have insisted that there is nothing supernatural about this enlightenment: The visions, ecstasies, and other alternative states of consciousness experienced by an adept are not a meeting with an alien, divine reality but are natural to the human condition, even though most people have not developed this spiritual potential within themselves. But the Buddhists also point out that, unless a man or woman has a special gift or potential, these techniques will not work infallibly. Zen masters insist no amount of teaching and practice will help people who are temperamentally or intellectually unsuited to contemplation. The guru or the spiritual director will have to tell the novice when he has reached the limits of his ability. Entering the depths of the mind can be extremely dangerous if the would-be mystic has not the mental or physical capacity for this interior quest. The higher states of consciousness cannot be attained by willpower and application. An unmusical person will be unable to progress beyond a certain point, no matter how many piano lessons he has. I myself discovered that I did not have this mystical ability, even though I spent seven years in a Roman Catholic convent, engaged in daily meditation and intensive spiritual exercise. This is difficult for people brought up in the Protestant tradition to accept, perhaps because Protestantism has always insisted that every single Christian has the ability to become a great spiritual athlete. Roman Catholicism has been more in line with the other great world religions in insisting that mysticism is only for a few chosen souls and that, unless one has this special propensity, mysticism can be a serious health threat. Its inaccessibility to the rank and file may be one reason why Protestants were, until the beginning of this century, extremely distrustful of the mystical experience.

If, however, a man or a woman has mystical ability, it will become essential. Mystics cannot be prevented from contemplation any more than a poet can be prevented from writing poetry. The compulsive drive toward a mystical mode of religion is particularly interesting in the three faiths of historical monotheism. It might seem that Judaism, Christianity, and Islam would find mysticism alien and difficult to incorporate. The mystic claims that the reality monotheists call "God" is essentially unknowable, but these revealed religions claim that he has spoken very clearly to men and that his divine Word has been expressed and can be experienced in very tangible ways. They are active faiths, dedicated to implementing the divine will in the world to ensure that God's will is done here on earth as it is in heaven, but the mystic withdraws from the world into his own psyche. Yet each of these monotheistic faiths developed its own distinctive mysticism, which was instinctively recognized by the establishment as an authentic — even an honored — spirituality, though relations with it are sometimes strained.

Indeed, the mystics played an extremely important part in each one of these three monotheistic religions, even though only a few people could undertake the mystical life. The mystics became an important elite, and their ideals and interpretation of the faith strongly influenced popular piety. Thus, in Europe, the mystical Kabbalism of Isaac Luria (d. 1572) had a deep and enduring influence on the thought and spirituality of Jews that has persisted to the present day, even though it may seem far in spirit from the Talmud. Sufism, the mysticism of Islam, was extremely influential in the Muslim world and became the dominant Islamic piety in many areas

of the empire until the eighteenth century. In the Greek
Church, the mystical writings of the fifth-century author who
wrote under the pseudonym Dionysius the Areopagite
achieved near-canonical status. Not only did they inform the
devotional and liturgical life of the people, but they also
influenced the development of Orthodox theology, which became hostile to any rationalistic or naturalistic ways of inter-
preting the reality of God and religious truth. Mysticism in all
these traditions gave the original revelation new life and significance. The revelation became a constantly repeated experience in the heart of the individual, instead of being
considered a definite historical event, a message delivered to
Moses, in Jesus, and to Muhammad that in effect put an end
to any further direct contact between God and men.

The development of mysticism in a particular tradition
represents a stage in the evolution of the religious consciousness. In his classic book *Major Trends in Jewish Mysticism,*
Gershom Scholem points out that it is incompatible with
certain earlier stages of religious development. In a pagan
world that was full of gods and where men and women
encountered the divine at every turn, there was no need for
the mystical disciplines to help people to cultivate a sense of
presence and unity: they already felt at one with the world.
But as society developed, men began to take control of the
world and felt their separation from it; instead of seeing
themselves as deeply identified with their environment, people became aware of the personality as perspicacious to itself
and as a unique, distinct entity. They became aware, therefore, of the vast gulf that separated them from the supreme
Reality, and the great confessional religions were born to meet
these new conditions. After the great divide had been ef-
fected, it was time for the mystics to find a new way to cross
the abyss and rediscover the old unity — not, this time, in the
outside world but in the depths of the self. Yet the utter

transcendence and separation of the Other remained a vital mystical theme: Mystics warned their coreligionists against the dangers of human projection and the creation of a new kind of idolatry by confusing ideas, concepts, and doctrines of "God" or the Absolute with the ineffable Reality itself.

Western Christians, however, took longer to reach this stage in their development than other traditions because of their peculiar historical circumstances. When Rome fell to the barbarian tribes during the fourth and fifth centuries, Europe was reduced to a primitive backwater. The Goths, the Franks, the Angles, and the Saxons had converted to Christianity, but in the absence of an effective establishment to instruct them in their faith it inevitably remained superficial. They still clung to many of their old pagan beliefs and practices. The Benedictine monasteries regarded themselves as islands of true Christianity in a sea of pagan barbarism, and it was not until the eleventh century that the monks of the abbey of Cluny and its affiliated houses began a campaign that was able to educate the laity and local clergy. The Cluniac reformers promoted the ideal of the pilgrimage, for example, as an external discipline that would help these new Europeans to cultivate an inner attitude. The long journey to a holy place where they would encounter the divine in a special way was a graphic demonstration of the Christian orientation to God; the hardships of the road, which rich and poor shared side by side, gave the pilgrims an impressive experience of community, charity, and poverty, with its rider: dependence upon God alone. By the end of the eleventh century, the Cluniacs really had begun to re-form the consciousness of Europe in institutions like the pilgrimage, and the West was ready to embark on its Age of Faith. The great cathedrals bore witness to a towering vision of transcendence yet, at the same time, expressed a confidence in the human ability to make the great leap necessary to bridge the gulf between heaven and earth.

In the early twelfth century, therefore, a distinctively Western spirituality was born. St. Bernard, Abbot of Clairvaux, developed a cult of inward sensibility that was unprecedented in Christian Europe, and his mysticism became the hallmark of the newly founded Cistercian order. Later in the century, Francis of Assisi began to develop a more romantic spirituality that took mysticism out of the cloister and into the world. But it was not until the fourteenth century, when Christian monotheism had really taken root among the people, that the people of Europe had evolved sufficiently to develop a widespread mystical tradition of their own.

The fourteenth century was a very turbulent period, however, and events proved that the people of Europe were on the brink of major social, political, and religious change. In the thirteenth century, Western Christendom had had to face the fact that their great holy wars against Islam, known as the Crusades had failed. Christians were driven out of the Holy Land of Palestine and had to acknowledge that they would never liberate Christ's tomb in Jersusalem from the infidel. They had invested a great deal in the Crusades, not merely monetarily but spiritually as well, and many felt that the integrity of Christianity depended upon a victory over the Muslim world. The failure of the Crusades had, therefore, caused immense distress and raised a crucial question: Why had God seemed to favor the enemies of Christ? This sudden failure of confidence was increased by events nearer home. In 1302, Pope Boniface VIII issued the encyclical letter *Unam Sanctam,* proclaiming that the Pope was the supreme head of Christendom and that his power was superior to that of the Kings of Europe. But only three years later, the Popes seemed to have deserted Rome, the see founded by St. Peter, chief of the apostles who was regarded as the first pope. Political troubles in Italy led the French pope Clement V to establish his court in Avignon, southern France, in 1305. In some ways, Avignon was a more rational center for Western Christendom than the more distant Rome, but human beings are not always entirely rational animals. Throughout Europe, men and women felt that the Roman Church had gone into exile and felt spiritually dislocated and that the world had shifted its central point of orientation. In 1377, therefore, Pope Gregory XI returned to Rome but died a few months later, only to leave the church with an even bigger problem.

The new pope, Urban VI, was so overbearing and rash in his behavior that in 1378 the cardinals elected another pope, Clement VII. For over fifty years there were two popes, a scandalous situation known as the Great Schism, which did immense harm to the church. Christians felt deep shame and disillusion. Not surprisingly, some felt that the papacy was permanently discredited and already reformers had appeared to challenge the authority of the pope. In 1324, Marsilius of Padua had argued that the Church should be ruled by general councils of bishops and that the state should control the papacy, and from 1375–82 the Englishman John Wycliffe attacked clerical wealth, the rich and powerful monasteries, and the authority of the pope.

England had its own troubles during the fourteenth century. In 1314, Scotland, under Robert Bruce, had broken away from the English crown and become independent. In 1327, King Edward II was driven from the throne and murdered at Berkely Castle. Edward III proved a more satisfactory monarch, but in 1337 war broke out between England and France, chiefly to liberate English feudal possessions in France from the French throne. In 1346, the English won a spectacular victory at Crécy but this only meant that Edward III was now committed to a war that would continue intermittently until 1453. The Hundred Years War, as it was called, was fought in France, but there were plenty of troubles in

England. In 1347, England, like her continental neighbors, was smitten with the horrific plague known as the Black Death, which, it has been estimated, wiped out between one-quarter and one-third of the population of Europe. This inevitably led to famine, as people could not farm the land, and to economic and social disturbance. This surfaced in England during the Peasants Revolt of 1381 when rebels from southern England, led by one Watt Tyler, advanced on London and demanded a more just government from the young King Richard II. They were fobbed off by Richard who persuaded them, on false pretenses, to go home, but rural insurrection continued until the end of the year. In 1399, Richard II, who had tried to rid himself and his friends from parliamentary control, was himself deposed and was either starved or smothered to death in 1400 in Pontefract Castle. During the fourteenth century, therefore, England had deposed and killed two kings and later English people looked back on the murder of Richard as a great sin. Shakespeare himself, in his cycle of history plays, saw it as the starting point of that dynastic struggle that resulted in 1455 with the outbreak of the civil war known as the Wars of the Roses, which cruelly tore England apart, turned families against one another, and caused death and widespread despair.

These painful upheavals seem to have inspired some people in Europe to look for a salvation that the external world could not give. Western Christians had now developed sufficiently to establish their own mystical tradition and begin the inner journey to a God found in the depths of the self. Throughout the fourteenth century great mystics appeared all over Europe. This phenomenon was particularly impressive in the north, which had hitherto been far less advanced and progressive than the southern, Mediterranean countries, the seats of ancient empires. The peoples of France, England, Germany, Scandinavia, and the Netherlands — which had previously been barbarous regions — had begun to catch up to the Greeks, Latins, and Spaniards and develop their own religious insights. St. Bridget of Sweden (1302–73) and the Fleming John Ruysbroeck (1293–1381) both independently founded cults that became influential in establishing the mystical life that would inform other religious traditions. Germany produced a veritable flock of mystics: St. Gertrude the Great (c. 1256–1302), Meister Eckhart (1260–1327), John Tauler (1300–61), and Blessed Henry Suso (1295–1306). Some were canonized and others — like Eckhart and Tauler — were hounded by the Church, but all were seen to be of enormous importance by their contemporaries, even by people who could not follow them into the inner world. They were the pioneers of a new human experiment in the West and seemed the men and women of the hour. It is perhaps not inappropriate to compare them to the astronauts in our own day: they had broken into an uncharted region, blazed a new trail to God and to the depths of the self, and had returned to earth like the heroes of antiquity, bringing news of a hitherto unimaginable realm that gave an entirely new perspective on the human condition.

England, too, made a significant contribution to this new Western development and produced four great mystics who quickly attracted a considerable following on the Continent as well as in their own country: Richard Rolle of Hampole (c. 1290–1349), the unknown author of *The Cloud of Unknowing*, Walter Hilton (d. 1376), and Dame Julian of Norwich (c. 1342–1416). We know very little about their lives, but we get a strong sense of the individuality of each one in their writings. Though some of them seem to have been familiar with the writings of some of the others, each worked independently and developed a personal view of the mystical life. But all addressed the themes that had also been crucial in other traditions. In their writings we also see the first attempt to express the reality of the mystical life in the English language.

It was a sign of the dawning self-consciousness of the age that more and more people were turning to the vernacular to express their deepest thoughts and feelings. Instead of reverting automatically to the universal European scholarly tongue of Latin, they were gaining a new confidence in the language of their own people. All four of our mystics wrote in what we now call Middle English, a language that had developed after the Norman Conquest and that grafted French onto the old Anglo-Saxon. It was used until about 1500, when it was superseded by Modern English, which was based on the dialect of the East Midland, used by Chaucer. Rolle, however, wrote his mystical treatises in Latin, even though he wrote his popular ascetical and ethical tracts in Middle English. It is a paradox — one of the many paradoxes of mysticism — that even though mystics insist that their experiences are radically ineffable, many of the greatest mystics have felt compelled to write them down and to try to communicate them to others. Richard Rolle and Dame Julian both wrote about their personal experiences, and both clearly felt that they had an important message to deliver to the world. *The Cloud of Unknowing* and Walter Hilton's *The Ladder of Perfection* were both manuals for novices in the mystical life and attempt to trace a coherent path through the nebulous and tortuous complexities of the inner man. Rolle tends to the lyric and rhapsodic, a style that does not cohere easily with the logical demands of Latin, but the other three all express the inexpressible cogently and methodically, with a calm that approaches these extreme states of mind quietly, shrewdly, and, sometimes, with irony and wry self-deprecation.

Our four English mystics may lack the imaginative and mythical depths of the great Kabbalists and Sufis, they may not be as daring and extreme as Eckhart, and they certainly do not have the lyrical passion of the sixteenth-century Spanish mystics St. Teresa of Ávila (1515–82) and St. John of the Cross

(1542–91), but they bear witness to the profundity and intelligence of the new English spirituality of their day. All claim that they are not writing for clever people, but this does not mean that theirs is the voice of a simple, unlettered piety. When they dissociate themselves from the academic world of their time, they are making the time-honored mystical point that what Wordsworth would call "the meddling intellect" had nothing to do with the vision of God. The mystic addresses a level of the mind and an apprehension of reality that is deeper and, perhaps, more archaic than the rational and cerebral.

But in fact all four were educated people. Even the incoherent Rolle had studied at Oxford — and possibly at the Sorbonne — in his unregenerate days, and Dame Julian, who calls herself "a poor, uneducated creature," was obviously familiar with scholastic theology and philosophy. Hilton was rooted in patristic and scholastic theology, and the author of *The Cloud of Unknowing* has been profoundly influenced by the writings of Dionysius the Areopagite.

The Cloud of Unknowing is, I have to admit, my favorite of the four mystical works anthologized here. I remember the excitement and relief I felt when I read it for the first time as a very young nun. After some years of struggling anxiously with the knotty complexities of Catholic devotion before the reforms of the Second Vatican Council, *The Cloud of Unknowing*'s stark insistence on the One Thing necessary was deeply liberating, and I felt that a weight had fallen from my shoulders. I soon discovered, of course, that this discipline was not as simple as it seemed — as indeed the author tirelessly points out. The *Mystical Theology* of Dionysius the Areopagite also dwells on a thick cloud of unknowing that separates the ineffable God from mankind, and this image dominated Greek theology. Even the most eloquent Orthodox theologians insisted that the ineffable God, a mystery that transcended all human words and concepts, must be approached in the darkness of silence. Jewish and Muslim mystics also emphasized the transcendence of the God who would never be known by the human soul in its entirety — even in the next world. Kabbalists even claimed that God *En Sof,* God as he is in himself, was not mentioned in either the Bible or the Talmud.

The Western tradition, however, has never subscribed to such an extreme theology of silence and unknowing. Western Christians have been more ready to ascribe qualities and attributes to God. Both Walter Hilton and Dame Julian insist that God is transcendent and cannot be described or grasped by the human mind, but they belong more to the Western tradition than the author of *The Cloud of Unknowing.* They are both deeply influenced by the theology of the great St. Augustine of Hippo (354–430), who had described the Trinity in psychological terms: just as the human mind, which was created in God's image, had three powers — memory, understanding, and will — so God's unity contained Three Persons, which corresponded to these human powers. The Greeks distrusted this theology, even though they had a deep respect for Augustine, because they thought that it was too anthropomorphic. But Walter Hilton and Dame Julian both demonstrate the rich spirituality that Augustine's theory could inspire. Some modern Christians may find the Trinitarian emphasis alien and difficult. The Trinity has remained the linchpin of Greek and Russian spirituality, but in the West it has tended to retreat to the sidelines and many find it an impossible concept: God is seen as One and Jesus often becomes a sort of divine, all too human friend in a vision that robs the Christian mystery of much of its transcendent power.

In the sixteenth century, the religious and political unrest that had troubled Europe for some two hundred years led to the phenomenon known as the Reformation. In Germany, the Augustinian monk Martin Luther, protested against the corruption and lack of spirituality in the Church, complaining that people had been misled into thinking that such good works as making a pilgrimage to a shrine, collecting "indulgences" to save them from suffering in Purgatory, or kissing the relics of a dead saint could save them. In fact, people could not be saved by their own merits, Luther argued, but only by God's freely given grace. He advocated a return to the Christianity of the New Testament and the Fathers of the Church. There was little new in Luther's theology, but the Church reacted so negatively that eventually Luther and his followers separated themselves from the Church of Rome. In Geneva, Switzerland, the French Reformer John Calvin also advocated a return to first principles and a purified Church structure modeled on that of the primitive Church. This new form of Christianity, which protested against the establishment, became known as "Protestantism."

This brief summary inevitably oversimplifies that immensely complex religious change that took place in sixteenth-century Europe. It has been explained in various ways. Some historians see it as a reaction against the corruption of the Church and to the aridity of current theology, but there is no reason to believe that this corruption was any worse than it had been for centuries. What was different was people's perception of it. Again, the reformation has been explained by the rise of the absolute monarchies in Europe, which shook off the sovereignty of the pope. Others see it as a result of the new individualism that was emerging in Europe. But none of these explanations can fully account for the changes. The Roman Catholic Church itself underwent a reformation of its own, that was expressed in the decrees of the Council of Trent and the spirituality of St. Ignatius Loyola and St. Teresa of Ávila. Europe was coming of age, and this meant that old religious and political institutions were no longer effective and had to evolve in new ways. The process had been evident way back in the fourteenth century, when the English mystics were exploring their inner worlds and working out a mystical salvation.

Many of these fourteenth-century mystics came from countries that would later become Protestant but it would be a mistake to see them as harbingers of Luther or Calvin. All four of these English mystics repeatedly declare their loyalty and affection for "Holy Church" and, again with the notable exception of Richard Rolle, had no problems with the establishment, even though, as we have seen, the Church was giving Catholics grounds for concern. People who are familiar with the work of the fourteenth-century English poets Geoffrey Chaucer and William Langland would be mistaken to imagine that their portrait of English religious life presents the whole picture. Langland's denunciation of a corrupt and venal religious establishment in *Piers Plowman* and Chaucer's ironical vignettes of hypocritical friars, lax monks and nuns, and pardoners selling indulgences are not the whole story. If this was the whole reality, it is surprising that the Reformation did not happen a good deal earlier. But the English mystics and their followers give us the other side of the picture. The fact that all won a following combined with their inspiring vision of Christian community shows that they also reflected a potent religious reality in their day. There was a new awakening to the life of the spirit and an intense interest in all religious issues. Far from there being a decline of fervor, there was more interest and deeper involvement in religion than ever before. By the sixteenth century, people were no longer willihg to put up with unsatisfactory Church officials. Lay men and women in particular were developing a personal spirituality that would ultimately enable them to form an independent view of theology and Church organization, and they would no longer have to rely on the educated establishment. In the fourteenth-century mystical awakening we see the first signs of that deeper and more committed type of religion that would finally culminate in both Protestant and Catholic reformations.

The English mystics, indeed, were interested in some of the issues that would later exercise the Reformers. All stress the role of grace and man's total dependence on God for salvation. They point out that good works are not the result of human willpower but are in some mysterious way the actions of God himself. Hilton links his mystical insight to traditional theology on this point. Like Luther and Calvin, he found a solution in St. Augustine. Like Calvin and his later disciples, Dame Julian agonized about the eternal damnation of those who are not numbered among the elect and struggles to square this with the goodness and love of God. These mystics are aware that the religious demands of the Church could induce a deep anxiety, which Luther certainly experienced. Buddhists call such anxiety an "unskillful state" because it can only embed a person in the ego he is seeking to transcend. Our mystics come to a similar conclusion and try to help their readers to develop a quiet confidence based on an imaginative vision of an overarching but indescribable benevolence that will ultimately make all things well.

Like art, religion is an imaginative and creative attempt to find a meaning and value in human life; despite the suffering that flesh is heir to, mysticism is a particularly interesting example of the attempt to interpret the faith in a new way; it discovers a new richness that was there in embryo waiting to be developed. But after the initial enthusiasm, mysticism in Europe waned somewhat. Perhaps because Western Christianity tended to express the faith in more rational and conceptual terms, mysticism never became as normative in popular and official piety as it did in other traditions. Later Western mystics remained isolated from the mainstream in their cloisters, and though they may have been regarded as saints, they and their particular religious ideals remained a minority form of Western Christianity.

The various reform movements of the sixteenth century were another attempt to adapt the Christian vision. The Protestant reformers wanted to return as far as possible to the spirit of primitive Christianity and looked askance at the mystical tradition, which seemed to have no warrant in Scripture. As they were also hostile to monasticism, wherein most mystics had their roots, they virtually abolished this particular type of spirituality in Protestant countries like England. Our four mystics had no successors; the type of spirituality they had developed for their countrymen was blotted out. The deeply egalitarian Puritan ethos could not stomach the idea of a mystical elite and promoted the idea that any Christian could gain an immediate experience of God. Radical sects like the Quakers, the Shakers, and the Methodists all encouraged the faithful to feel the divine in tangible forms; some Pentecostal sects would speak in tongues, hear voices, or experience powerful feelings that came upon them with such force that they were believed to come from God. But this type of spirituality has nothing to do with mysticism. As we shall see, mystical teachers tirelessly proclaimed that visions and voices were not an essential part of the mystical journey and could in fact be a distraction; the mystical apprehension of God certainly had nothing to do with the ordinary emotions. Poets and artists would see the world in a visionary light. Thus, Thomas Traherne (1637–74), William Blake (1757–1827), and William Wordsworth (1770–1850) were all visionaries in this sense, seeing the world as informed by a presence, piercing the veils of the commonplace to glimpse another order of being. But none of these visionaries descended into the depths of the self to find God there or confront the apparently impassable gulf between God and the world as our mystics do. It was not until Evelyn Underhill and Dean Inge began to consider mysticism seriously that Anglicans started to see it as a spirituality that was authentically Christian.

In some ways, the modern experience of psychoanalysis resembles mysticism. Both can only be undertaken with expert guidance, both make a journey to the depths of the self, and both claim to experience a deep liberation that unlocks hidden reserves of power. More and more people are turning to this type of therapy and are discovering in it many of the consolations and insights that had once been the preserve of religion. Today we have less confidence than before in the power of more external, socially oriented ideologies to change the world. We have watched the demise of enthusiasms like nationalism, Marxism, and Thatcherism, which promised a salvation of sorts. Many people feel that a deeper solution is necessary and seek the interior transformation of psychotherapy or counseling. In the late twentieth century, therefore, people may find the mystical experiment, which also urges the adept to look within himself for the truth and warns against the danger of simplistic ideas and projections about God, to be a more attractive form of religion than the more conventional and dogmatic types of faith.

1

Richard Rolle
of
Hampole

ichard Rolle's conversion to the solitary life tells us a good deal about his spirituality. Born at the end of the thirteenth century in the Yorkshire village of Thornton-le-dale, he studied for some years at Oxford, sponsored by Thomas Neville, Archdeacon of Durham. At that time the Oxford course lasted seven years, and Richard left before taking his degree when he was nineteen years old, feeling, as he explains in his mystical treatise *The Fire of Love,* that his youth was being wasted on worldly and dissolute pursuits.

Accordingly he returned home to Yorkshire with the firm intention of becoming a hermit. But, not surprisingly, his father was not sympathetic to this idea and Rolle decided to run away. The *Legenda,* the lesson for the special Office that was composed in Rolle's honor after his death, tells us what happened next:

> *After he had returned from Oxford to his father's house, he said one day to his sister, who loved him with tender affection: "My beloved sister, thou hast two tunics which I greatly covet, one white and the other grey. Therefore I ask thee if thou wilt kindly give them to me, and bring them tomorrow to the wood near-by,*

together with my father's rain-hood." She agreed willingly, and the next day according to her promise, carried them to the said wood, being quite ignorant of what was in her brother's mind. And when he had received them he straight-way cut off the sleeves from the grey tunic and the buttons from the white, and as best he could he fitted the sleeves to the white tunic, so that they might in some manner be suited to his purpose. Then he took off his own clothes with which he was clad and put on his sister's tunic next his skin, but the grey, with the sleeves cut out, he put over it, and put his arms through the holes which had been cut; and he covered his head with the rain-hood aforesaid, so that in some measure, as far as was in his power, he might present a certain likeness to a hermit. But when his sister saw this she was astounded and cried: "My brother is mad! My brother is mad!" Whereupon he drove her from him with threats, and fled himself at once without delay, lest he should be seized by his friends and acquaintances.[1]

A new hermit was supposed to get a license or a blessing from his bishop, but Rolle had no time for these forms. His spiritual life would follow the same unorthodox and aggressively assertive pattern.

Rolle is said to have fled to the nearby village of Pickering, where the squire John de Dalton was impressed by the strangely clad hermit and agreed to support him and give him an anchorage to live in. Rolle did not stay with him, however. As he tells us himself, he frequently fell out with his patrons and became a peripatetic solitary, roaming from one place to another. The *Legenda* tells us about a few miracles that he is supposed to have performed, but otherwise he seems to have lived a fairly uneventful outward life. He ended up in the village of Hampole near Doncaster, where he became the spiritual director of the local anchoress Margaret Kirkby, who lived a solitary life in a cell next to the church, and the nuns of the Cistercian convent. He died in 1349, probably of the plague known as the Black Death. Miracles were performed at his tomb, and until the Reformation there was a cult of St. Richard the Hermit there.

Rolle made a great impression on his contemporaries. We will see that the author of *The Cloud of Unknowing* and Walter Hilton both warn people against the dangers of his kind of mysticism. All sound mystics insist that the experience of the divine has nothing whatever to do with emotion and certainly nothing at all to do with physical sensation. Many of the disciplines of contemplation have been designed precisely to wean the mind and heart away from these earthbound modes of perception to help them to discover another kind of experience, which they call "spiritual." To stay and luxuriate in ordinary emotions and sensations means that the contemplative is trapped in our normal limitations. A mystic has to learn to transcend these by means of the special techniques and carefully cultivated attitudes, which his spiritual director must teach him.

Not only did Rolle not have a spiritual director, but he had absolutely no intention of getting one. He was convinced that he had no need of human advice because he was instructed directly from within by God himself, who made his presence felt in strange but delightful experiences. Few mystical treatises get off to a more intriguing start than *The Fire of Love*, which describes the first time Rolle became aware of a heat in his breast that, he insists, was not imaginary or metaphorical but that could be felt as a finger felt the heat of the flames into which it had been thrust. Rolle fingered his chest in consternation, trying to work out where this strange warmth had come from, but soon decided that it was from God, because it brought with it a flood of pleasurable and consoling emotion. His treatise was an attempt to argue that, despite what his critics said, this kind of religious experience was not only valid but a sign of God's special favor.

Rolle also claimed to hear a heavenly music that was inaudible to the outward ear but real enough to make any church music absolutely intolerable to him. This music, which sometimes came with the heat in his chest and sometimes separately, also released a flood of pleasurable emotion that Rolle identified with the love of God.

This miraculous experience was far more appealing to many of his contemporaries than the sober, austere disciplines of the more conventional mystics. But though Rolle's manifest sincerity is not in question, his account would have given many people cause for concern. The mystical life should carry a health warning: it can seriously damage your mental and physical health. Plunging into the subconscious is risky: you never know what you will find in there. That is why mystics in all religious traditions insist that this journey must not be undertaken without the close guidance of an expert. *The Cloud of Unknowing* repeatedly insists on the necessity of taking expert advice from a spiritual director at every stage. The spiritual director or guru played a role that is similar to that of an analyst today, who leads his patients safely through the perilous regions of the psyche.

In *The Fire of Love* Rolle emphasizes the joyful aspects of his experience, and his excitable, intense religiosity gives the reader the impression that he was on a perpetual — even a manic — "high." In one telling passage he speaks of his loneliness and of a crushing depression. Why, he asks God, has he never sent him a friend who would have been able to make sense of his inner experience and translate the "music" he has heard in his soul into intelligible sound? A good spiritual director would have been able to interpret this experience and lead him, step by step, past these dangerous swings of mood to a disciplined equanimity that was rooted in a deeper part of the self and that was not so dependent upon exterior circumstance.

It is no accident that in all the great religions, people who want to engage in this kind of contemplative activity have organized a monastic life to cater to their needs. Details and emphases differ from one culture to another, but the similarities are evident. The withdrawal from the world, the silence, the disciplines of community, and the deliberate cult of monotony in a system where everybody wears the same clothes and does the same things day after day have been found to support the mystic during his frequently lonely journey, to ground him in reality and to wean him away from an excitement and drama that is inimical to the mystical experience. All religions have had their solitaries too, but the greatest of these usually made sure that they had a spiritual adviser and some kind of structure. This provided an element of stability to counterbalance the mental extremity to which they were continually exposed.

Rolle, however, was a freelance and, as we see in his headlong flight from home at the beginning of his vocation, discipline had no place in his spiritual quest. Nor did compassion, consideration, and respect for others. In all traditions, the iron rule of contemplation is that the mystic must be able to integrate his experience successfully with his daily life. A disorderly, uncontrolled, and egotistic lifestyle is a very bad sign indeed. The mystic is seeking to transcend his ego and acquire a disciplined compassion — a crucial virtue in all religions. Rolle, alas, must fail this test. He is often an engaging writer: he is blunt and sometimes disarmingly frank about his attitudes and dealings with others, but there is a stridency and arrogance that jars with the lush descriptions of his joy in the love of God. He certainly doesn't have to submit to normal disciplines: Nobody at all should presume to criticize him, and people who do not understand his religious experience are fools! His prose is highly mannered in both his Latin and his English treatises; it calls attention to itself and to the writer in striking contrast to the calm, lucid prose of our other mystics, who are all careful to make it clear that their word is not law but only their own opinion.

A true mystical experience is not only intended to make the adept less egotistic, but it should also make him more alert and help him to function better. A spiritual discipline should not make a practitioner lose control, become vague, dreamy, and inept in his daily life: eccentric or uncontrolled behavior is a sign that the mystical experience cannot be integrated with the mundane. But all religions have had their mystical failures who have used their experiences to prop up the ego rather than transcend it and whose behavior has been very odd indeed. Rolle's great contemporary St. Catherine of Siena (1347–80) once fell into the fire when she was in ecstasy though she was supposed to be cooking a meal. That is precisely the sort of dangerous and unhealthy state that the mystic is cautioned to avoid. Catherine's problem was that she was an extremely clever woman with a real talent for mysticism, but she never found a spiritual director who was either intelligent or knowledgeable enough to control her and lead her beyond this perilous psychic hinterland.

Rolle also hints that he might have been damaged in some way. He says that somebody who experiences the fire of love will find that he is affected physically. He may find that he develops a stammer and is unable to speak quickly or clearly anymore and that his whole body has slowed down. A job that once took half an hour will now take a whole morning. More experienced mystics, like the author of *The Cloud of Unknowing* and, later, St. Teresa of Ávila, continually warned their readers against these kinds of unhealthy physical and emotional states. They are nothing but "foolishness" or "egotism." No true contemplative must indulge this kind of behavior. Continually adepts are warned that they must not strain themselves or try to experience these unnatural things. Both

The Cloud of Unknowing and Walter Hilton suggest that some
people who had read Rolle's work or who had heard about his
experiences were almost breaking all bounds in order to feel
something similar themselves and were, consequently, damaging themselves as well as wasting their time.

It is tempting to think of Rolle not as a mystic but as a
charismatic or Pentecostal Christian. This type of spirituality,
which relies on feelings and even on bodily experiences like
trance or speaking in tongues, has nothing to do with mysticism but is an entirely different type of religious experience. It
can also — though by no means always — result in a similar
egotism and aggression. Charismatics can be very dismissive
and intolerant of those who do not share their religious perspective, and Rolle frequently reminds us of such an attitude.
He might have been more at home in some of the radical
Protestant sects that began to appear in England and —
later — in America during the seventeenth century.

It is also possible, perhaps, that Rolle was a musician
manqué. He may well have heard in some reach of his mind an
as yet uncreated harmony, as a composer hears the music that
he is about to translate into sound. The music Rolle "heard" in
this way could have been quite out of its time and incomprehensible to medieval ears. If this was in fact the case, it makes
Rolle's aversion to church music more understandable. In the
small village churches where he worshiped, the singing and
organ playing was likely to be intolerable to somebody with
an acute musical sensibility.

In Spain, the Jewish mystic Abraham Abulafia (1240–
c.1291) had propounded a mental discipline that he compared
to the science of harmony and music. To wean himself away
from concrete, physical sensation, the Jewish adept should
learn to contemplate language in a way that would divorce it
from meaning and physical reality. He was to combine letters
of the Hebrew words of a text into new arrangements that,

Abulafia said, produced a sensation that was similar to listening to musical harmonies, the alphabet taking the place of notes on a scale. But this was a music of thought, not sound, and its purpose was to stimulate an alternative state of consciousness. Abulafia used the phrase "to untie the knots" to describe this process of getting beyond our normal sense-perceptions — it is a phrase that is also used in Tibetan Buddhism. In a rather similar way, mystics in certain sects of Shiite Islam — like the Druze — use mathematics, a science that is akin to music, as a way of weaning the mind from the physical to the abstract in the preliminary stages of meditation; it is a first stage in the long, disciplined process of discovering a different mode of perception.

Rolle, however, allowed his "music" to tie him all too firmly to normal sense perceptions and unregenerate ways of thought. We can see this in his outrageous behavior toward his three women patrons: He seemed quite surprised to learn that touching a woman's breasts is not what is expected of a hermit and, when rebuked, concludes that it is better to keep clear of women altogether since they veer so erratically from love to contempt. The reader cannot avoid the impression that this is a classic case of projection of one's own failings on to somebody else! In his ultimate rejection of women, Rolle is quite different from the other three mystics, and, indeed, some of the most distinguished of the fourteenth-century mystics were women. Yet for all his failings, Rolle acquired many followers. *The Cloud of Unknowing*'s author describes the strained antics of those who had embarked on an unhelpful quest for sensational experiences and weird states of mind. He may well have had Rolle in mind. It is salutary to begin our exploration of English mysticism with Rolle, because he reminds us that the mystical experiment could lead the unwary into all kinds of spiritual and physical dangers, to an uncharitable rejection of others or to a sterile solipsism.

The Fire of Love

Prologue: Richard's First Experience of This Divine Fire*

I can't tell you how astonished I was when I felt my heart grow warm for the first time. It was a real warmth, too, not an imaginary one: I seemed kindled with a fire that I could feel with my senses. I was astonished by the way this heat broke out in my soul, bringing with it a rich consolation that I had never experienced before. I kept feeling my chest over and over again to see if this burning sensation had a physical cause. But when I realized that it came entirely from within myself and that this fire of love had no sensual or sinful origin but was a gift from my Creator, I melted with joy and wanted my love to increase still more, especially because of the pleasurable sensations of interior sweetness that poured into my soul with this spiritual flame. Before my heart had been flooded by this devotion, which was more comforting than any other I have experienced, I did not think it was possible to feel such divine warmth during this exile of ours. It set my soul ablaze, as though a real fire were burning there.

*The chapter headings throughout this book are Karen Armstrong's.

But, as others have said, there are certainly people who are afire with love for Christ, because it is clear that they thoroughly despise the world and devote themselves whole-heartedly to the service of God. But I am arguing that a loving soul feels a heat that is as real as that felt by a finger that is thrust into the fire. Sometimes this is more intense than at others, sometimes less, according to the capacity of each fragile soul. For who could possibly survive this heat if it blazed all the time at the highest temperature — the highest that we can bear in this life, that is? Anyone would be bound to faint if exposed to the sweetness and immensity of such excessive love and indescribable heat. But at the same time he will find that he is also bound to yearn for this fate. He will want to breathe out his soul, adorned as it is with so many marvelous gifts, in this honey-sweet flame and die, leaving the world behind in order to be snatched at once into the company of those who sing the praises of their Creator.

But things happen that fight against this love, when sordid fleshly matters erupt in our souls and destroy our peace. Our bodily needs and strong human affections break into this warmth during our difficult exile here below and disturb and quench this flame, which I have described with the metaphor of fire because it burns and sheds light. These distractions cannot take away something that has been fixed permanently, and my heart has been completely penetrated by this love. But because of these temptations this joyful warmth does disappear for a while, and until it comes back I am spiritually frozen and feel abandoned, because I have got used to this consolation. During this waiting period, I am longing to recover the consciousness of that interior fire that my whole self, body and soul, welcomes with acclaim and that brings it security.

Besides these other distractions, even sleep has become my enemy: I resent the time I have to devote to sleep. While I am awake, I try to warm my dark and cold soul up again. I know the way to set it ablaze when it is weak in devotion and lift it above the things of this world with a mighty longing. But when I am asleep this rich and endless love does not come to me and I feel no spiritual ardor when I am worn out after a journey; nor does it happen when I am too busy about worldly business or involved in ceaseless arguments. I find myself growing cold on those occasions, until I put all outward matters behind me and try to stand in the presence of my Savior. Only then do I retain this inner warmth.

I am not, therefore, offering this book for philosophers or the wise men of the world to peruse; nor is it for important theologians who are caught up in never-ending controversies, but for the simple, unlearned people who try to love God rather than amass a heap of information. For God cannot be known in theological debates but in our deeds and our love. Even though the matters discussed during such disputations demand a high degree of intellectual ability, I don't think that they are nearly as important as the love of Christ. Who can understand them, anyway? So I have decided not to write for these clever people, unless they have put aside and forgotten every worldly concern and are ablaze with longing to surrender to God, their Creator. First they must flee all worldly honor, they must hate all showy scholarship and desire of acquiring a reputation, and then, by submitting to a very poor life and with prayer and meditation they can devote themselves continuously to the love of God. In this way, a little fire of uncreated love will doubtless appear within them and this will prepare their hearts for the fire that consumes all darkness and will raise them to that peak of fervor that is so lovely and pleasurable.

Then they will leave all time-bound things behind and sit enthroned in infinite peace. The more learned they are, the greater will be their ability to love as long as they despise themselves and are glad when other people look down on them. And so, because I want to inspire everybody to love God by using these methods and am trying to explain the supernatural nature of this burning and ardent love, the title I have chosen for this book is *The Fire of Love*.

From Chapter 4: God's Lovers, the World's Lovers

There isn't a single human soul who will be able to experience the fire of endless love unless he first forsakes all worldly ideals with the firm intention of studying heavenly things. He must long for the love of God ceaselessly, but he must also give to each created thing the love that is its due. For if we love everything for God's sake, we love God in it rather than the thing itself, so it follows that we do not take delight in the creature but in God — in whom we shall rejoice and glory for ever. But wicked people want to enjoy this world here and now: it becomes the object of their affections and they are always looking for things that will bring them earthly satisfaction. Can there be anything more stupid, pitiful, and destructive than to cling to things that are, by their very nature, decaying and doomed to pass away?

For God, the Trinity, must be loved for himself alone. Let us consecrate our minds wholly to him. Let us try to refer all our thoughts to him, their final end, so that he may be glorified in us forever. Let us love ourselves and all the other creatures we love for his sake alone.

A sinner who claims to love God but is not afraid to be the slave of sin is a liar. Everyone who loves God is free and is not fettered and enslaved to sin. Such a man controls himself and devotes himself to the service of goodness without hesitation. When we love worldly things and earthly comforts for their own sake we certainly do not love God. On the contrary, if we take such pleasure in created things, we ought to be accounted the enemies of God rather than his servants, because we are putting other things above their Creator and have lost interest in the desire and quest for eternal things. There is no more dangerous moment for a soul — and it is a sign of its everlasting damnation — than when a man surrenders wholly to this world, to sensual desires and to other kinds of error, as if he were free to take whatever path he chooses. No doubt about it, such a pitiful wretch is destroyed at the very time he is living this enjoyable life. While he imagines that he is wallowing in pleasure, he is really rushing straight to hell.

So nobody should have the nerve or presume to boast about his high rank; but neither should he defend himself when he is treated with contempt or when people hurl insults at him. He ought to accept everything with equanimity — praise as well as abuse. If we really behave like this we shall rejoice forever with our Creator, provided that we love him ardently and incessantly during our time on earth. This love for him, once rooted securely in our hearts, transforms us into his likeness and with this fervent love another kind of transformation — a divine glory is poured into our souls.

For his love is a fire that sets our hearts ablaze so that they glow and burn, purifying them from all the dross of sin. Blazing in his chosen souls, this fire compels them to gaze continually in spirit toward heaven and to cultivate a constant longing for death. In the meantime, while it is still possible for us to sin, let us concentrate on fleeing worldly prosperity and putting up joyfully with adversity. For the sinful mind is perishing even in the midst of its pleasure, and as long as it looks for happiness in created things, it is killing itself with an alluring poison. We must make every effort to avoid this contamination by preserving our taste for that spiritual food that is reserved in heaven for those who have loved God fervently.

And so, with Christ's permission, let us find comfort in the songs of love and take our pleasure in the sweetness of piety, while the wicked fall asleep in a fearful darkness and, stuffed with sin, are sinking toward their doom. It seems quite obvious that a mortal man is ravished by this kind of love for God, because in his heart of hearts he really only finds comfort in heavenly things and, like a soaring organ voluntary, he rises up and achieves his high ambition to contemplate God. He transforms all the things that others use to hurt him into glory, so that his soul seems quite proof against suffering. Even the fear of death has no power to disturb him, and nothing whatever can shake his equilibrium. Now that he is inspired by this imperative love and his mind is fixed continually on Jesus, he is quick to recognize his own faults, to correct and avoid them. And so he lives a consistently good life until the time comes for him to be led to his God to sit with the heavenly creatures on an everlasting throne.

From Chapter 5: Love Over Knowledge

Of all the things that we are obliged to undertake or that engage our minds, let us choose to love God rather than to acquire knowledge or engage in theological disputations. Because it is love that fills the soul with delight and makes our conscience sweet by drawing it away from inferior pleasures and from the danger of seeking our own advantage. Without love, knowledge cannot build us up or help us to achieve salvation; instead it just puffs us up so that we become wretched and lost. Our soul must have the courage to take on difficult tasks for God's sake, therefore, and the knowledge that we acquire must be flavored with heavenly rather than worldly things. It yearns to be enlightened by the Eternal Wisdom and to be fired with that sweet flame that causes us to long for our Creator and to love him alone. The warmth of this love gives us the strength to spurn everything that passes away with all our hearts. . . .

So let us make sure that the love of God is ablaze within us. This is a more worthy ambition than taking part in pointless arguments. For when we hurl ourselves into an untrammeled and curious quest, we inevitably lose the sweet, pleasurable experience of heavenly things. Too many people these days burn with such an ardent desire for knowledge instead of love that they are wholly ignorant about the nature of love and its special flavor. But really all their study should have been directed to this end so that they too could be kindled by the love of God. What a shameful thing! An old lady can be more of an expert in the love of God and far more unworldly than a theologian despite his useless learning, because he studies out of vanity, in order to enhance his reputation and to acquire a salary or a high position. A man like that deserves the title of "Fool" rather than "Doctor"!

Chapter 6: We Cannot Understand God

A rich, integral, and holy truth is revealed to those who seek it, and inaccessible mysteries are open to those who cherish and preserve the divine unity. What is the reason for the undisciplined mentality of a heretic, which looks for things that are of their very nature beyond them, blinded by a hunger for personal reputation? Indeed, because of their empty desire for the wrong things, they never stop fighting against God. They openly resist the truth in their plausible arguments, even though the Christian religion urges us to cut away anything harmful to it and that the community be united in the truth. Heretics and other arrogant people are endlessly begetting new ideas and spreading opinions that depart from the traditional teaching of the Church. They positively seem to enjoy destroying those things that faithful Christians hang on to with unshaken faith, by means of their trivial ideas.

We regard their errors as contemptible. The Son of God is coeternal with the Father. We must always believe this and understand it correctly, because if the Father had not begotten the Son from all eternity, the Son would not have been wholly divine. For if there had ever been a time when God did not have a Son, it is not exaggerating to say that God would then be a lesser being then than he became later when he begat a Son. No sane person can make this claim! The God who cannot change begets the unchangeable God: he begets him from all eternity and still continues to beget him. Because the essence of the Begotten cannot be described as "begotten" on only one occasion, nor can the essence of the Begetter be known apart from the Begotten, who was generated by him. Indeed, the origin of the divinity cannot be discerned by either reason or intellect, precisely because it did not have a beginning. Thus, too, the Begetter of the Son remains unchangeably in his eternal divine nature. And truly when the wonder and majesty of God shines forth only in infinity, without any beginning, who would be fool enough to claim familiarity with a mystery that cannot be spoken to our mortal ears? The person who knows God fully is one who recognizes that God is incomprehensible and unknowable, far beyond our capacity.

For we cannot know anything completely unless we also fully understand its origin and its nature. But in this present life "we know only in part and we understand only in part."[2] But in the next world we shall know fully and perfectly, insofar as created beings are capable of knowing and if such knowledge is beneficial to them. But anybody who is hungry for a knowledge of the eternal Creator that can only be harmful to him must be an idiot, who is mentally defective. "What is God?" you ask, and I make this brief reply: "His nature is such that nothing greater or better exists or possibly could exist." But if you ask again "What is God?" in the hope of getting a more accurate knowledge, I tell you that you will never find an answer to your question. I do not know; the angels don't know and even the archangels haven't heard the answer! So how can you seek to know what is essentially beyond knowledge and cannot be conveyed to anyone? Even God himself, who can do all things, cannot teach you what he is. For if you knew what God is you would be as knowledge-able as God himself, which is way beyond your ability as a mere creature. Stay in your proper place, therefore, and do not try to get above yourself, because if you want to know what God is you want to be like God — and you know quite well that that is entirely inappropriate! Only God knows himself or has the ability to know himself. But God's inability to teach you what he is in himself is not due to a weakness on his part but it is due to his inexpressible splendor, because he is not able to be other than he is. If he could really be fully known, he would not be beyond our understanding. So it is enough for you to know *that* God is; it will only hold you back if you seek to know *what* he is.

And it is, therefore, an admirable thing to know God fully, that is, to realize that he is incomprehensible. To recognize him in this way is to love him, and to love him like this is to rejoice in him. Rejoicing in him is to rest in him and to arrive at eternal rest and inner tranquility. Don't be worried because I have told you that you must recognize God perfectly though I have also denied that you are able to know God. "Show your mercy to those who know you."[3] To keep clear of error, you should understand the words "to those who know you" in this way: those who know God are those who know that you are a God who must be loved, praised, adored, glorified; the only Creator of all things, who is above all things, pervades all things and is in all things, blessed be he for ever and ever, Amen.

Chapter 11: The Music of God

Nothing can satisfy the human soul but God, because it has a capacity that only God can fill. That is why the people who love this world are never satisfied. The peace enjoyed by those who love Christ is a consequence of the fact that their hearts are fixed with yearning and consideration of the love of God, and they contemplate him as they sing with ardent love. This peace experienced by the spirit is very sweet. A divine and dulcet melody comes down to fill it with joy. The mind is ravished with this sublime and effortless music and it sings the joys of everlasting love. The praise of God and the Blessed Virgin, in whom he glories more than he can tell us, resounds from his lips once more. There is nothing odd about this, for the heart of the singer that pours out this praise is ablaze with fire from heaven. And he is transformed into the likeness of him who is all sweet song and he is drunk with his lovely passion for the taste of heavenly things. He rejoices in the warmth of his love. People who are dead through and through cannot understand this at all and an outsider cannot imagine how a man in a corruptible mortal body can experience anything so sweet and delectable. But it even astonishes the person who receives this gift, and he can only rejoice at the indescribable goodness of God who gives liberally and is slow to scold.[4] It is from God that this experience comes. Moreover, once he has experienced this immense gift — and it is truly immense and beyond the ken of those who are dead in their sins — he is never happy without it but is always pining with love. Meanwhile, he remains constantly on guard and sings and meditates on his love and his Beloved. If he is alone, he is even more absorbed in his song.

But actually somebody who has received this experience once finds that it never wholly departs from him afterward because a trace of that passion, song, or sweetness remains behind, even if all three things are not present to the same degree at the same time. They are all there, nevertheless, unless this person is overwhelmed by a serious illness, is stricken with a heart attack, shattered by severe hunger and thirst, or paralyzed with cold, heat, or by a journey. So it is better for somebody who wants to sing his love for God and rejoice fervently in this song to live alone. But he should find a happy mean between excessive abstinence and luxury. Provided that he does not realize what he is doing and has the good intention of keeping his body alive, it is better for him to take more than he needs rather than become weak because of excessive fasting and so too ill and physically frail to sing. But it is certain that somebody who has been chosen for this vocation is never overcome by the wiles of the devil, whether he eats or abstains, because somebody who really loves Christ is instructed by Christ himself and does not waste time whether he has too much or too little food. He will merit far more by singing happily, praying, contemplating, reading, meditating, and by eating sensibly too than if, without any discretion, he was always fasting and eating only bread and herbs during his prayer and study. That is why I myself have eaten and drunk things that are regarded as delicacies — not because I love these things but to enable my body to keep going in the service of God and in the joy of Jesus Christ. It was better that I conformed my lifestyle with that of the people I was living with, rather than imagine that I possessed a virtue that I didn't and so caused men to praise me excessively when I really didn't deserve much praise at all. I have left people, however, not because they fed me badly but because our lifestyles were not compatible or for some other sensible reason. But I dare to say with the blessed Job: "Fools despised me when I left them and they turned against me."[5] Nevertheless, people who say that I refused to stay in a place where I was not fed on delicacies will blush when they meet me face-to-face. For it is better to see what I scorn rather than to long for something that I do not appreciate.

Fasting is extremely effective in repressing the carnal desires of the flesh and in gaining mastery over an uncontrollable, chaotic mind. But the false and fleshly desires of fallen man are practically extinct in a person who has reached the heights of contemplation with joy and burning love. A man who gives himself over to contemplation has sentenced all evil desires to death because his inner self has been transformed into a glory and to a model that is quite different. He does not live in himself anymore: it is Christ who lives in him.[6] Hence he is absorbed by this love and is overcome by his longing for God. He almost faints away because of its sweetness and can scarcely live because of this love. This is the soul that says: "Tell my beloved that I am pining away with love."[7] I am longing to die, yearning to be annihilated, burning to pass into a new existence. Look, I am dying of love! Come down, Lord! Come, my Beloved, and soothe my longing! Look! I am in love, I sing, I burn! I am ablaze within! Have mercy on my pitiable state and give orders for me to come into your presence!

He who possesses this joy here below and glories in it during his lifetime has been inspired by the Holy Spirit. He cannot wander into a false path. He is safe and free to do whatever he likes. No mere mortal can give him such good advice as that which he has within him from the eternal God. Other people who want to give him advice will undoubtedly make mistakes because they do not understand all this. But even if he really wants to submit to their advice, he himself will not go astray because God will not allow it. God holds him firmly in his will so that he never goes beyond it. Of such people it is said: "The spiritual man judges all things and is himself judged by no man."[8]

But nobody should take it upon himself to assume that he is himself such a man, just because he has wholly renounced the world, is meticulous in his pursuit of the solitary light, and has reached the heights of contemplation. This grace, indeed, is not granted to all contemplatives but only rarely and to very few people who have reached the supreme haven of body and soul and who are set apart simply for the task of loving God. It is difficult to find such people because they are rare birds: they are cherished, sought out, and loved by God and men, and even the angels are delighted when they leave this world because they are more suited to the company of angels. There are, on the other hand, many people who offer their prayers to God with great devotion and sweetness and who are able to taste the delightful experiences of contemplation in their prayer and meditation, but they do not advance any further and remain in this peaceful state.

From Chapter 12: Richard Learns from Three Women

Lord God, have mercy on me, my infancy was silly, my boyhood pointless, and my adolescence impure. But now, Lord Jesus, my heart has been set on fire with holy love and my disposition has changed so that my soul no longer wants any contact with those bitter things that had once been my food and seemed sweet to me. My enthusiasms now are such that I hate nothing but sin, fear only to offend God, and find no joy in anything but God. My only grief is sin, my only love is God, my only hope is in him. Nothing makes me sad but wrongdoing, nothing pleases me but Christ.

But in fact there was a time when I was quite properly rebuked by three women. One rebuked me because in my zeal to correct women's insane enthusiasm for extravagant and voluptuous dress, I gazed too closely at their numerous ornaments. She said it was not right for me to notice whether they were wearing horned headdresses or not. I thought that she had reprimanded me quite correctly, and she made me blush.

The second rebuked me because I spoke of her huge breasts as if I liked them: "What business of yours is it if they are big or little?" she said. Again, she was quite right. The third jokily took me to task when I made as if to touch her a bit rudely — perhaps I had already touched her — saying, "That's enough, brother!" It was as though she had said: "Playing around with women doesn't suit your office as a hermit." She also made me feel embarrassed, quite rightly. I should have controlled myself rather than behaved like that. When I came to myself, I thanked God for teaching me that their reprimands were correct and for showing me a more agreeable path than the one I had known before so that I could respond more wholeheartedly to the grace of Christ. In future I am not going to put myself in the wrong with women.

A fourth woman whom I knew rather well did not reprimand me so much as speak to me with contempt: "You're only a pretty face and a lovely voice: you haven't actually *done* anything." So I think it is better to do without them, whatever their specialty is, than to fall into the hands of women. They don't know how to preserve a happy mean: it's either love or contempt! But these things did not happen to me because I was after anything improper, but because I was attending to their salvation. In fact they were the people from whom I had received my food for a while!

Chapter 15: Solitary Life

When adolescence arrived during my unfortunate child-hood, the grace of my Creator was also with me. He curbed the lusts of my body and transformed these into a longing for spiritual intercourse. He raised my soul up from the pits and translated it to the heights so that I yearned for the delights of heaven more than I had ever enjoyed carnal embraces or the depravities of the world. The way this happened, if I intended to publish it, forces me to preach the solitary life. For the Spirit breathed into me and intended me to pursue this life and to love what it set out to do. From that moment, despite my weaknesses, I tried to put this insight into practice.

I still lived apart from people who were successful in this world, however. I accepted their food and I listened to the flattery, which can drag the most doughty warriors from the heights down to hell itself. But when I put all this aside in order to pursue the one thing necessary, my soul was caught up in the love of my Creator. I yearned to enjoy the sweetness of eternity and I set my soul to the discipline of loving Christ, and she has received this gift from her Beloved so that now it is solitude that attracts her most, together with all those other consolations that misguided men dismiss as nothing.

In fact I became accustomed to look for quiet, even though I went from one place to another. For it doesn't hurt a hermit to leave his cell for a good reason, nor to return to it again if that seems the right thing to do. Some of the holy fathers used to do this and were criticized for it — though not by good people. For evil people said evil things and would have translated these into evil actions if the fathers had stayed in the same place, for that is the way that such people behave. In the same way, take people who speak from an overflowing heart and there you find the poison of asps! I know that the more people have raged against me with their crazy slanders, the more progress I have made in the spiritual life. The worst detractors I have had have been people whom I once considered to be faithful friends. But I did not give up the things that were proving to be helpful to my soul because of their accusations, but I pressed on with my effort and always found that God looked after me. I recalled that scripture that said: "Let them curse you, but you should bless,"[9] etc. And in due course I was granted an increase in spiritual joy.

From the beginning of the conversion of my life and mind to the time when the gate of heaven opened and God's face was unveiled so that I could gaze upon the things above with the eye of my soul and see the way it could find the Beloved and cling to him incessantly, three years less three or four months passed. But when the gate had opened, it was another year before I actually felt the warmth of eternal love. I was sitting in a certain chapel, delighting in the sweetness of prayer and meditation, when I suddenly felt within myself an unusual but pleasant warmth. At first I did not know where it came from, but I soon realized that it did not come from one of God's creatures but from the Creator himself, because it was a more ardent and pleasurable feeling than I had ever experienced before. But it was half a year and three months later before a perceptible and inexpressibly sweet and glowing heat passed through my belly together with an infusion and apprehension of heavenly spiritual sound that belonged to the song of eternal praise and to the sweetness of a melody inaccessible to normal hearing. This sound cannot be known or heard by anybody but the one who receives it, and he has to keep himself pure and separate from the world.

While I was sitting in the same chapel and was chanting the night psalms before supper to the best of my ability, I heard above me a resonant psalmody or singing. I was straining toward heaven in my prayer with a concentrated desire, when I gradually sensed in some indescribable way a choir of

singers and I could hear within myself a similar heavenly
harmony, which was utterly delightful and which lingered in
my mind. Then suddenly my thoughts were transformed into
song, my meditation became an ode, and my own prayers
and psalmody reverberated with the same heavenly sound.
Because of the abundant sweetness within me, I immediately
began to sing when before I had only spoken, but I sang in a
hidden way and only for the ears of my Creator. The people
who saw me had no notion that this was happening, because
if they had found out they would have given me too much
honor and I should then have lost a part of this lovely flower
of devotion and fallen into desolation. In the meantime I was
astonished that I should have been rapt in such joy while still
in exile and that God had given me gifts that I had not even
realized I could ask for and that I thought could only be
given to a very holy person in this life. For this reason I
believe that such gifts are not bestowed as a reward but are
given freely to whomsoever Christ chooses. But I still don't
think that anybody will receive them unless he has a special
devotion to the Name of Jesus and reveres it so much that
he never lets it pass from his mind, except when he goes to
sleep. Anyone who receives this latter grace will, I am sure,
achieve the other also.

Four years and three months passed from the beginning
of my conversion to the moment when, with God's help, I
managed to reach the highest degree of the love of Christ.
When I had attained this height I filled the air with the praise
of God and with joyful singing. And after these first occasions,
this blessed state has endured with me and will continue to the
end. Indeed, after death it will be still more perfect because
though this joyous love and fervent charity begin here below,
they are gloriously consummated in the Kingdom of Heaven.
But someone who has passed through this stage during this

life enjoys no little advantage, but he does not advance to a higher degree. No, indeed, because he has, as it were, been strengthened in grace and is at peace, as far as a mortal man can be. Thank God for this: I long to praise him without ceasing. He has comforted me when I was in distress, in my troubles and when I was being persecuted, and he has given me the confidence to expect an eternal crown during periods of prosperity and success.

So, Jesus, I want to be free to praise you incessantly. This is my joy. When I was nothing and a mere pitiable wretch you found me worthy and allowed me to mingle with those sweet ministers from whom the beautiful and heavenly melodies flow. I will thank you and rejoice tirelessly because you have made me one of those souls who make music with a pure conscience. Such a soul is burning with endless love. He is aglow, transfigured. He burns with fire and indeed he seems to expand because of the intensity of his desire. Surely virtue that is beautiful, true, lovable and faultless blooms in the presence of my Creator. His song fills his whole being: its joyous melody makes his burden easier to carry and it brightens his toil.

There are many marvelous and great gifts here on earth, but none of them can be compared to this one, which strengthens our hope in that unseen life within the loving soul. It consoles him with its sweetness when he sits in prayer and it snatches him up to the highest peak of contemplation and to the sound of the angels' songs of praise.

So, brothers, you see that I have told you how I came to the fire of love not to make you praise me but so that you might glorify God from whom I have received all the good I possess. I intended that you, who understand that "everything under the sun is vanity,"[10] should be inspired to imitate me instead of pouring scorn upon me.

From Chapter 19: Love of God and Neighbor

If you appreciate beauty, you must realize that this qual-ity will cause you to be loved by the Highest Beauty of all, provided that you keep your love undefiled, for the love of him alone. For all physical beauty is corruptible, frail, and contemptible. It passes away so quickly and deceives all those who love it. Virtue in this life consists in this: that we should cleave to the truth and refuse to be separated from it, once we have despised the world and trampled vanity underfoot. All the visible things that people desire here below are empty, but the things that we cannot see belong to heaven and they will endure forever. Every true Christian shows that he has been chosen by God in this way: he reckons the things of this world as nothing; he knows that only his longing for divine gifts will enrich him, and from these he receives the hidden and sweet music of love. Nobody ever gets to know this music by means of earthly love, because while a man wallows in carnal lust he has, he is, alas, far removed from any taste of spiritual plea-sure. But, as one might expect, the shining soul who is wholly intent on the love of the Eternal and follows Christ tirelessly is usually overflowing with sweetness, according to the capacity of his heart. It sings its joyful song, even in this fleshly life, as though it were already living with the angels.

So provided that our heart is pure and perfect, whatever delights it is God himself. Indeed, as long as we love ourselves and all the other creatures who are worthy of God's love simply for his sake, what else are we in love with but God? For when we love God with all our heart and mind, we are certainly loving our neighbors and all other lovable things at the same time. And this is as it should be. So if we enter God's presence and pour out our hearts in love of him, binding ourselves to God and clinging to him, what other love is possible to us?

For in the love of God is the love of our neighbor. It follows, therefore, that just as a person who loves God finds it impossible not to love man, so too someone who truly loves Christ can be proved to love only God in him. And so we give back to God, the source of all love, everything that inspires our love and all that we love. For he who demands that everybody must be devoted to him, also wants every emotion and impulse of our minds to be intent on him. Indeed, somebody who is really in love with God feels that there is nothing in his heart but God alone, and if he feels that there is nothing else there, he truly has nothing else. He loves all the things he has for God's sake and only loves the things that God wants him to love. It follows that he has no love for anything but God and so all his love *is* God.

Indeed, the love of such a person is true love, because he conforms himself to his creator, who made everything for his own sake, and therefore God also loves everything for God's sake! When the love of eternity has really been kindled in our souls, all worldly triviality, all the lusts of our flesh seem the vilest dung. And for as long as a mind that is completely dedicated to piety seeks only the good pleasure of the Creator, it wondrously bursts into flame with the ardor of love. Little by little it makes progress and glows with spiritual gifts. No longer is it stumbling down the broad, slippery road that leads to death, but it has been lifted up to the contemplative life with a fire from heaven and marches stoutly, climbing higher and higher.

In this vale of tears, nobody is going to become perfect in the contemplative life all at once. First, a man's heart has to be set entirely ablaze with the torch of eternal love, so that he feels it burning with heavenly love and realizes that his conscience has melted with a honeyed sweetness. It is not surprising that when a man first becomes a true contemplative, that is, when he tastes this sweetness and actually feels this warmth, he nearly dies with a love that is more than he can bear. He is held tight in the embrace of eternal love, as though it was physical, because with ceaseless contemplation he is striving with his whole heart to climb to see that infinite light. Eventually such a man will not allow his soul a comfort that does not come from God. He is pining with love for him and strains and pants for the end of this present life, crying anxiously with the psalmist: "When shall I come and appear before the face of God?"[11]

This is the perfection of love. But once this state has been attained, can it ever be lost? That is a proper question to ask. For as long as a man has the ability to sin, it is possible for him to lose charity. But to be incapable of sin is not the condition of those of us who are still on the road, but only of those who have reached their homeland. So however perfect a man becomes in this life, he still has it in him to commit even a mortal sin. For, as everybody can vouch, the appetite for sin is never entirely extinguished in our traveler. Somebody who never felt any temptation whatever would obviously belong more to our heavenly homeland than to this life, because he would be faultless if he was unable to sin. I myself have no idea whether there is any such person living in the flesh because — and here I speak only for myself — "the flesh lusts against the spirit and the spirit against the flesh and though I delight in the law of God according to the inner man,"[12] I still do not know whether my love is strong enough to quench all lust completely.

From Chapter 23: Sex and the Love of God

Nothing should be loved apart from the good it possesses or is thought to possess, whether this is real or apparent. That is why people who love physical beauty or worldly riches as ends in themselves are deceived. For in visible objects that we can touch there is never the pleasure that appears to be on the surface, nor the glory that they seem to represent, nor the fame that people want to acquire.

No spiritual neglect is more damnable than when a man gazes at a woman to lust after her. For once this glance has set him on fire, in no time at all he will start thinking about the lady he has seen and this awakens lust in the heart and ruins the interior man. At once he is enveloped in the smoke of a noxious fire, which prevents him from seeing the sentence of the presiding Judge. For the soul is cut off from the sight of heavenly things by an impure and malignant love and is bound to show the signs of its damnation outwardly. It identifies its well-being with the consummation of this unclean desire it has conceived, and so immediately sorrow is born in this vile lust. Lust gives birth to sin because the more a man is fooled by the great peril that threatens his soul — which he tries not to see — the more quickly he falls into filthy pleasures. He never gives a thought to the judgment of God. As soon as he begins to entertain these thoughts of carnal pleasure, he takes no notice of the miserable abyss into which he is plunging. God has judged that somebody who has freely chosen to set God at naught and falls into mortal sin will be damned in the next world (this time, against his will!). That is what God has decreed. In the world to come, such a man will not be able to save himself from the sting of Hell because during this life he abandoned himself to crime and sin at every opportunity. He did not want to abandon them; he did not even begin to do so.

From Chapter 31: Richard Describes the Trouble He Has Had from His Enemies

Because various men and women are duly appointed to sing the praises of God in church and to inspire devotion in the congregation, I have often been asked why I don't want to sing like the others, because people often see me at High Mass. They thought I was on the wrong track and argued that everybody ought to sing aloud to their Creator and make music that everybody else could hear. I did not reply, because these people were entirely ignorant of the kind of songs I sing to Christ, my Intercessor, and of the sweet harmonies that I put forth. They imagined that no one could hear this spiritual song, simply because they themselves didn't understand how such things could be. But it is absurd to assume that somebody who is totally dedicated to God cannot receive a special gift from his Beloved, just because they have not experienced anything like this.

That is why I thought that I should make some kind of answer, so that people who argue like this do not have things all their own way. Is it any of their business how other people live their lives — people whose way of life is in many ways superior to their own? People who know far more about the unseen world than they? Can't God be allowed to do what he likes? "Are their eyes evil because he is good?"[13] Do they really want to reduce the will of God to their own limited standards? Is it not true that all men belong to God and that he can choose the people he wants and reject the rest, he who gives whatever he wants to whomsoever he wishes, whenever he chooses? Whatever he does, he always shows his immense benevolence!

My guess is that the reason these people grumble and make false accusations is that they want people who are better than they are to come down to their own level and conform to

their inferior standards. They think that they are superior
when in fact they are the underdogs. And so my soul plucked
up the courage to tell them something about that music that
rose up from the fire of love and that I sing to Jesus, and
throbs with the sweetest harmonies. But then they attacked
me even more fiercely because I tried to avoid the external
and audible songs that are usually sung in church and the
organ pieces that the congregation listens to. They also complained that I only heard Mass when I had to — I had no
choice in this matter — or when it was an important holy day
in order to prevent the slander and bitter attacks of the
people. All I have ever wanted to do was to sit and concentrate on Christ and on him alone. That was why he gave me
this spiritual song, as a means of offering praise and prayer to
him. The people who argued with me did not agree with this
and tried to make me conform to their form of worship, but I
could not possibly abandon the grace of Christ and give in to
stupid men who had no understanding of my inner life whatsoever. I put up with their talk and did what I had to do,
according to the state in which my Lord had placed me.

I mention this and give thanks and glory to Christ so
that there will be an end to this kind of idiocy among people,
this presuming to sit in judgment. What I have been doing
has not been inspired by a fantasy or as a joke, as some
people interpret my actions. It is true that many people are
deceived and believe that they have been given something
that they have not, but an invisible joy really has come to me
and I really have been warmed within by the fire of love,
which has lifted my heart far above these lesser matters. I
now rejoice with Jesus, leaving the external melodies far
behind, and enter the song within my soul.

Besides hating things that contaminate and rejecting the
empty words of other people, I have also tried not to eat more
food than necessary and at the same time not to discipline

myself excessively — even though I have been said to be addicted to the houses of the rich, to indulge myself at table and
to be a *bon viveur*! But through the grace of God, my soul is
ordered quite differently: it takes delight in the things of
heaven rather than delicious tidbits. Since that time I have
never ceased to love solitude. I have chosen to live far from
men, as far as my physical needs permit, and I have received
one consolation after another from my Beloved.

From Chapter 32: The Way of Love

Someone with a vocation, who has chosen to love
Christ alone, transforms himself into his Beloved. He has no
worldly possessions and he does not want to own anything,
but he follows Christ in voluntary poverty and lives content-
edly on the alms that others give him. He has a clear conscience, sweetened with a heavenly savor, and he pours out
his heart in love for his Creator. Every day he tries to
increase and lose himself in his longing for heaven. Everyone
who renounces the world and genuinely wants to be in-
flamed by the Holy Spirit will take care that he does not let
himself grow cold in prayer and meditation. For in this way
and by the tears that accompany his prayers as well, indeed,
as Christ's grace, the mind is kindled with a marvelous love.
Once it has been kindled, it rejoices and, rejoicing, it is
raised to the contemplative life. The soul that is in this
exalted state flies far away; snatched beyond itself, it discovers that the heavens have opened and offer their secrets
to its inner eye.

But a man must first work very hard at his prayer and
meditation for a few years, barely taking time out to attend to
the needs of his body. By ardently applying himself to prayer,
rejecting any false ideas, he does not weary in his quest for the

experience of divine love, night and day. This is how the
Almighty Lover inspires new love into the one who loves him
and raises him up to a spiritual peak far above the things of
this world and the clamor of vain, vicious thoughts. Now "no
dead flies destroy the sweetness of the ointment,"[14] for they
have all vanished. And finally the love of God will become
sweet indeed and he will be intoxicated with its subtle sweetness; he will taste this miraculous honey until he is aware of
nothing within himself but the consoling infusion of this flavor, which is a sign of the highest sanctity. Anointed with this
sweetness, he will strive to remain vigilant, because anyone
who feels his heart aflame with the fire of eternal love is
certainly not going to allow his mind to turn away from this
enlightenment, this sweet mystery. . . .

A person who loves the Godhead, whose whole being is
saturated with love for the Beauty that we cannot see, rejoices
in his inmost being. He is gladdened by that entrancing fire
because he has dedicated himself wholly to God. And so,
when Christ wills and not by virtue of his own deserts, he will
receive a sound that descends from heaven into his heart. His
meditation will be transformed into a song and his mind will
dwell in this wondrous harmony. . . .

Now at this point, something happens to the lover that I
have never found in any learned texts or heard explained.
That is, that this song springs to his very lips and he will sing
his prayers in a spiritual symphony of heavenly sweetness; he
will find that when he tries to speak he can only stammer
because he is slowed down by the abundance of his inner
happiness and the peculiar nature of this song. Something
that previously would have taken him only an hour, he can
now scarcely finish in half a day. While he is receiving this
heavenly song, he will sit by himself and mix as little as
possible with those who are singing psalms and will deliberately avoid singing with the others. I am not saying that

everybody should attempt this, but let somebody who has
received this gift do what he wants, because he is led by the
Holy Spirit and his life is not going to be put off course by the
words of mere men!

Moreover, his heart will be living in brightness and fire
and he will be lifted above himself by this astonishing music.
He will not take any notice of the status of men, even if he is
considered a simpleton or a bumpkin. He will praise God in
the depths of his being with jubilant song: this praise bursts
out aloud; his most sweet voice rises up to heaven and our
Divine Majesty loves to hear it.

A man whose beauty is desired by the King has a comely
face because he possesses the uncreated Wisdom within himself. For his wisdom is drawn from a hidden source and she is
enjoyed by those who are in love with eternity. She is certainly
not found here on earth by people who lead indulgent lives,
but she lives in the kind of man I have been talking about,
because he has been totally absorbed into the love of Christ
and his whole inner self cries out for God. This cry is his love,
his song, and he raises a great shout that reaches God's ears.
This enthusiasm for perfection constitutes the longing of a
good man. His is not a shout of this world, because he is
yearning only for Christ. His inner being is ablaze with the
fire of love: his heart is lit up and burning. He engages in no
external task that cannot be turned to good. He praises God in
a jocund song — but in silence! His odes are not for the ears of
men, but he utters his songs of praise in the presence of God in
inexpressible sweetness.

From Chapter 33: The Great Shout

There is one way by which a man who has been raised to
holiness can find out whether he possesses this song I have

been describing, namely, that he cannot stand the noise of psalm-singing unless his own song is mentally in tune with it. It is ruined if he has to speak outwardly. It is true that some people become distracted in their singing and psalmody, not because they have achieved perfection but because they have restless minds and the words of other people interrupt their prayers and confuse them. This sort of thing does not affect the perfect man. People whose piety is well-founded cannot be distracted from prayer and meditation by shouting or noise or by anything else: these things only shatter this song. For this sweet spiritual song is very special indeed and only given to very special people! It has nothing in common with that ordinary physical singing that is used in churches and other places. It clashes horribly with all outward sounds made by the human voice and with physical noises that we hear with our ears. It is only among the choirs of angels that it finds something that it is in harmony with, and people who have experienced this song describe it with astonishment and approval.

So, you men, look and understand! Don't be deceived because, for the honor of Almighty God and for our own convenience, I have shown you why I used to run away from singers in church and why I did not like to mix with them and chose not to listen to the organ playing. These were an obstacle that got in the way of this sweet sound; they forced these magnificent songs to die away. So don't be surprised if I ran away from something that would have destroyed me: I would have been wrong not to have left something that I knew would deprive me of the most beautiful song of all. I would have been at fault to have done anything else. I know from Whom I received it and I have tried to submit perfectly to his will, in case he should take from this ungrateful wretch a gift that he had so generously bestowed upon him. . . .

But people who have got their learning from books

instead of receiving it directly are puffed up by their compli-
cated theories and ask scornfully: "Where did he get this
from? What teacher has he been listening to?" They do not
believe that those who are in love with eternity can be instructed by a Teacher within, so that they speak far more
eloquently than people who spend their entire time studying
for empty degrees. But if the Holy Spirit inspired so many
people in the olden days, why should he not raise up today
those who love him to let them gaze upon the glory of God? —
especially since some of our contemporaries are deemed not
unequal to the men of the past? Yet I don't call mere human
opinion "approval," because men are often wrong in what
they approve: they choose people whom God has rejected and
reject his chosen ones! The people who are really approved
are inwardly aflame with eternal love.

From Chapter 34: The Effects of Love but Richard Is
Lonely and Isolated

It is both fitting and reasonable that somebody who loves
the Almighty should be caught up to contemplate higher
things in his mind and to give utterance to the song that surges
through his soul, which is ablaze with the fierce, bright fire of
love. This fills him with sweet devotion. His entire being is a
hymn, which breathes the fragrance of his Savior's sweetness.
As he sings he is led on to an experience of total delight and,
with this well of fervor bubbling up in his soul, he is taken into
the sweet embrace of God. He is overwhelmed and enriched
with the most intense ardor when this singular comfort comes
to him and he is crowned with the highest blessings. He shines
whiter than snow and glows more redly than a rose because
he has been set alight with God's flame. Adorned with a pure
conscience, he walks in white garments. He has been taken up

above other men almost in secret, because of the melody that is ever in his heart and the abundant, sweet fervor that remains with him. He not only offers himself wholeheartedly as a sacrifice while he praises Christ with his spiritual music, but he also urges other people to love him so that they rush to give themselves to God with total dedication. For anybody who loves Christ and clings to him with all his heart will be given joy during his exile, because the delicious taste that the love of Jesus brings to him transcends any experience we have here below and I cannot even describe the smallest part of it adequately.

For who can describe a fervor that is ineffable? Who can lay bare such infinite sweetness? I know that if I wanted to speak of this inexpressible joy, I would seem as though I were trying to empty the sea, drop by drop, bit by bit, and push it down into a tiny hole in the ground! It is no wonder that I, who have scarcely tasted a drop of this towering experience, cannot disclose the immensity of this eternal sweetness. Nor is it surprising that you, with your blunted perceptions and distracting fleshly thoughts, are incapable of taking it in, even if you are clever and intelligent and zealous in the service of God. . . .

And so the lover who is fired by these spiritual caresses and who is purged of all sordid and passing thoughts that distract him from the one thing necessary strives with all his power to gaze upon his Beloved. And then, bursting from the source of this yearning love, his shout ascends to the Creator, though it seems to him as though he were calling from a long way away. He raises that interior shout, which is only found in the most ardent lovers. Here I find myself inarticulate because of my usual stupidity and dullness. I am simply not able to describe the shout itself, its mighty power or even the pleasure that comes just from thinking about it, feeling it, or experiencing it. I cannot tell you about it now, nor will I be able to do so in the future, because I do not know how to rise above the limitations of my sensuous experience unless I simply tell you that the shout is the song.

Who is there to sing the music of my songs to men, express the joys of my passion with ardent love and the warmth of my youthful longing, so that from this society of warmth and song I might at least seek out my essential nature? Or so that the degree of music that I have deemed worthy to receive might be made known to me? Or that I might find that I had been freed from my unhappiness? There are things that I cannot presume to claim for myself, since I have not yet found what I hoped for, but I might be able to enjoy them in the sweet comfort of a friend.

If I really thought that that shout and that song was entirely hidden from my outward ears — which is what I am actually trying to make clear — I would give anything to find someone who was experienced in this melody. Once he had written down that unspoken music, he would be able to sing my joy to me and bring forth to the light of day those spiritual notes and songs that I have not been embarrassed to bring into the presence of my Beloved, in his Name, which is above all others. Such a person would be more precious than gold to me and I would not find a single one of the valuable things that we treasure during our exile equal to him. For the charm of virtue would be manifest in him and he would really be able to search out the secrets of love. In a word, I would love him as I love my own heart and it would never occur to me to hide anything from him because he would reveal the song that I am longing to understand to me. He would make my joyful shout clear and plain. The more I understood, the more I would exult and the more fruitful would be my imitation of him. For the fire of love would then be shown clearly to me and my song would shine out distinctly, so that everybody would be able to see. My babbling thoughts would not struggle without anybody to turn these into praise, and I would not toil in vain. But as it is, I am totally exhausted by my exile and my problems weigh so heavily upon me that I can scarcely keep going. And at the same time as I am inwardly aflame with uncreated heat, outwardly I am skulking miserably, to all appearances depressed and in the dark!

So, my God, to whom I offer all the devotion of my heart, won't you remember me in your mercy? Because I am a poor wretch and I need your mercy. Surely you will raise up into your light the yearning that holds me in its grasp, so that when the time is right I shall have what I long for. You will transform the toil by which I make reparation for my sin into a mansion of delights, so that melody may live in the former abode of sorrow and I will see my Beloved whom I desire in the grace of his beauty. I am pining for him, and once I have been clasped in his embrace I would praise him for ever and ever, for He is the one I desire.

Chapter 37: Rapture

To those in whom the beauty of God has inspired a longing, their passion of spirit reveals a pure love. Such a person wants nothing but his Beloved and all his other affections have been totally extinguished. So his mind is now freely borne to what he loves so sweetly and the union of their wills is strengthened and made firm. Nothing can now hold the lover back from his project or make him think again, so that, in the supreme happiness of love, he can take his desire to himself and with the last obstacle down, he can rush into the arms of his Beloved.

Among all the other delights he is experiencing, he becomes aware of a heavenly secret that has been incorporated into his sweet love and that is known only to him. The special pleasure that intoxicates the joyful lovers of Jesus is at work within him; this drives such people more speedily on their way to the heavenly thrones, where they will enjoy the glory of their Creator forever. They are yearning for this, intent on the things above. On fire within, their inmost being rejoices to be enlightened by such magnificent delights. They seem to be transported by this delectable love and absorbed into this marvelously joyous song.

The experience makes their thoughts as sweet as honey, while they go about their business here below. Because whether they are studying or meditating on Scripture, or writing or debating, they think continuously of their Beloved and this praise that is habitual to them is never diluted. You might find it astonishing that one mind can do two things at once and attend to each one at the same time. That is, the mind offers and sings its love to Jesus, rejoicing in a way that is its own, and at the same time it can understand what is written in the books and neither activity clashes with the other!

But this grace is not given to everybody indiscriminately, but only to the holy soul, steeped in sanctity, on whom shines the highest love and in whom hymns inspired by Christ well up spontaneously, so that in an indescribable manner she reverberates with joyful song in the presence of her Creator. Now it is that the soul realizes the mystery of love and rises up to her Beloved with intense delight and with a great shout. Her intelligence is most penetrating and acute at this time, her perceptions most refined. The mind is not scattered in this worldly matter or that, but everything is entirely recollected and integrated in God and established there. The soul serves God with a pure conscience and with a shining mind, and she has vowed to love him and surrender to him.

The more pure the love of this lover, the closer is God's presence, the purer his joy in God, the richer his experience of God's goodness, benevolence, and sweetness. For these are the things that God likes to infuse into those who love him and to slip into the hearts of his devout servants with an incomparable joy. Love, moreover, is only pure when it has not been diluted with a desire for anything else, however trivial, and when there is not the slightest inclination to take pleasure in physical beauty. That would not do at all. His piercing mind has now been purified and is totally established in its desire for eternity. Now that he has been liberated spiritually, he looks constantly at the things that are above, like one who has been snatched away from the beauty of all other things. He will not incline toward them and he cannot love them.

Now, it is clear that the word "rapture" can be understood in two ways. The first is when a man is rapt beyond all bodily sensation, so that at the time of his ecstasy it is obvious that his body feels nothing and he is physically helpless. He is not dead, however, but alive because his soul still gives life to his body. Some of the saints and the elect have experienced a rapture like this for their own edification and to instruct other people. Paul, for example, was rapt "into the third heaven."[15] Even sinful people sometimes experience this kind of rapture in a vision, where they see the joy of the blessed and the punishment of the damned to make them amend their own and other people's lives, as we have often read.

But the second type of rapture comes from the raising up of the mind to God in contemplation, and this is the way for all the perfect lovers of God — and only for them. It is just as correct to call this a rapture as the other, because it is just as extreme and beyond our natural experience. It must be a supernatural action when some vile sinner is transformed into a child of God and is borne aloft to him, full of spiritual joy. This second type of rapture is more desirable and lovely, because Christ perpetually contemplated God like this, but this did not make him lose his self-control. So one way is to be rapt in love while retaining physical sensation and the other way is to be rapt out of our senses in some vision or other, terrifying or pleasant. I myself think that the rapture of love is preferable and more of a reward, for to be granted a vision of heaven is a gift of God: we cannot merit it.

Those people can also be called "rapt" who are wholly and completely wrapped up in their Savior's will: they deserve to rise to the highest contemplation. They are enlightened by the uncreated wisdom and deserve to feel the warmth of that Light by whose beauty they have been seduced. This also occurs when the love of God enables a devout soul to set all her thoughts in order and when her wandering mind has become stable and she no longer wavers or hesitates. Instead, led on by her love for one thing only, she sighs for Christ, reaching out for him, and is as intent upon him alone as though only two things existed: God and her loving soul. Joined to him by the unbreakable bond of love and flying from the prison of the body in ecstasy of mind, she drinks deeply from the chalice that is more wonderful than we can imagine. She could never have achieved this unless the grace of God had snatched her from her feeble desires and planted her on this spiritual peak where she receives the gifts of grace.

So when she deliberately sets her mind only on divine and heavenly things, her heart now liberated and unshakable, she finds that her mind has been carried away and rapt to heaven, far above all the material things that we can see. Now, without any doubt, she is about to receive and experience within herself the warmth of love and will shortly melt away in a song as sweet as honey. For this follows rapture in the soul who has been chosen. That is why rapture is such an immense and wondrous thing and, I believe, superior to our other activities in this life. It is considered to be a sure foretaste of the sweetness of eternity. Unless I am mistaken, it surpasses all the other gifts that God bestows on the saints to reward them during our pilgrimage on earth. For they deserve a higher place in heaven because they have loved God with more fervor and quiet. The very greatest quiet is required to discover and hold on to such love, because if there is too much motion, restlessness, or mental indiscipline it can be neither received nor retained. When one is chosen, therefore, and raised up to this state he lives in great joy, is very virtuous, and dies in sweet security. In the next world, he will be even more distinguished among the choirs of angels.

In the meantime he has this sweetness, warmth, and song, which I mentioned earlier at some length, and by means of these gifts he serves God and, loving God, clings to him and refuses to be separated from him. But because this corruptible body burdens the soul and our earthly dwelling place inhibits our experience with its busy thoughts, he is not always able to rejoice as easily as this nor sing with the same clarity and constancy. Sometimes his soul feels the warmth and sweetness more strongly, and finds it difficult to sing. And then, when she [his soul] is about to sing, she is rapt in a wonderful sweetness and ease. But when this warmth is diminished she will often fly off with the greatest pleasure into song, and realize that in ecstasy the heat and sweetness are truly with her. For there is never heat without this sweet delight, though it can sometimes exist without song because any physical singing or noise can impede it and drive it back into reflection. But they are more clearly present in solitude, where the Beloved speaks to the heart. He is a bit like a timid lover who cannot embrace his girlfriend in front of everybody and won't even address her familiarly but acts as though she was just like anybody else to him — even a stranger.

The devout soul who has definitely severed himself from all alien pursuits and desires with all his heart to enjoy only the caresses of Christ, pining ardently for him, will soon arrive at the sweetest joy. Melody flows from him and brings a marvelous pleasure to his soul. She takes this as a sign that in future she will not normally be able to stand any exterior sound, for this music is spiritual. Nobody who is absorbed in worldly matters knows anything about it, however lawful or unlawful their business. Nobody has ever known it but he who has made the effort to keep himself free for God alone.

From Chapter 40: The Love of God

The love of the Godhead wholly penetrates a man and truly sets him aflame with the fire of the Holy Spirit; it takes the soul to Himself with wondrous joy and does not allow him to forget this love for a second. It binds the mind of a lover so that he is not concerned about trivial things but is wholly intent on his Beloved.

If we really love our Lord Jesus Christ we can keep him in our thoughts while we are on a journey, for example, and hold on to our song of love while we are in company. We can remember him at meals, even while we are enjoying our food and drink. But we ought to praise God with every morsel or sip we take and in the intervals between morsels and meals, we should sing his praises in our minds with honeyed sweetness, and mentally cry for him with desire, yearning for him even during meals. And if we are working with our hands, what is there to prevent our heart rising up to heaven, clinging to the memory of eternal love? So we can be fervent and not lazy at every moment and only sleep will take our heart away from him.

Oh, what great joy and happiness is poured into the lover! Oh, what happy and desirable sweetness fills his soul! For when love is fixed and established in Christ it will always endure. Neither prosperity nor adversity can change it, this loving desire that has its roots in heaven, as the wisest scholars have written. For without doubt, it turns night into day, darkness to light, sorrow into melody, punishment to pleasure, and toil to the sweetest rest of all. For this love is not a fake or a fantasy but real and perfect, intent on Christ and inseparable from him, and it resounds with harmonies and love songs. And indeed if this is the way you love, as I have shown, you too will be with the best and most distinguished in the Kingdom of God, you too will be in glory and granted that life-giving vision. In the meantime, you will bravely overcome all the assaults of the devils, all our carnal temptation and all desire for the things of this world, because of your fervent love and the power of your prayer. You will also conquer your delight in beauty that is only apparent, because you will not want even a single stain to arise from your thoughts. Indeed, you will be overflowing with inner nourishment and you will experience the pleasures of eternal love so that you know beyond any doubt that you are the lover of the eternal King. But none of this happens to anyone unless God gives it to him or unless he realizes that even here below an important part of his future reward is already dwelling within him.

But why do I talk about all this with other people who may be chosen but who do not yet possess this choicest gift? I sometimes marvel at myself because I have spoken of the high state of the lovers of God as though anybody who wanted could attain it. In fact, it is not for somebody who wants it or who hastens after it, but for him whom Christ has loved and raised up and who takes this love into himself. Indeed, my puny mind did not know how to explain what I was trying to explain in my incoherent way, but I felt compelled to say something about this ineffable matter so that those who hear about it or read it can make the effort to imitate it and find that divine love, which makes all the most beautiful and lovable things of this world seem like pain and grief.

Consider this intelligently, therefore, and know how this astonishing God creates his lover, how he carries him up to the heights, refuses to let him be cast down by unworthy love or empty hopes, but keeps him safely in himself to be loved most sweetly. For love is a continual meditation with an immense longing for what is beautiful, good, and lovely. For if anything I love is beautiful but not good, I am obviously not fit to love. If, however, it is also good, it must be loved.

II

The Author
of
The Cloud
of Unknowing

hen I was about eight years old, I had to learn this answer to the question: "What is God?" in the Roman Catholic catechism: "God is the supreme spirit who alone exists of himself and is infinite in all perfections." It was an answer that did not mean much to me then, and I confess that it means very little to me today. It is not only a rather arid and pompous definition, which seems to drain the idea of God of imaginative life, but it also seems arrogant — even hubristic. The compilers of the catechism seemed to have no doubt that it was perfectly possible to define God and say precisely what he is. The author of *The Cloud of Unknowing* gives a much more honest, humble, and thought-provoking answer to the question "What is God?" He simply replies that he hasn't the faintest idea.

It is sometimes suggested that the mystical flowering of the fourteenth century was a reaction against the scientific and scholastic enthusiasms of the thirteenth century, which had sought to reinterpret the Christian experience in terms of the rationalistic philosophy of Aristotle. This, as we shall see, is not quite true: some mystics were inspired by scholastic ideas. But St. Thomas Aquinas (1225–74), the leading scholastic theologian, is said to have had a reaction against the spirit of his work. There is a story that when he had dictated the last sentence of his monumental *Summa Theologiae,* he laid his head in his hands sadly. When the scribe asked him what was wrong, Thomas replied that everything he had written was straw compared with what he had seen. The Greek Orthodox Church had earlier reached the same conclusion. The Greeks regarded rational discussion as the lowest and least reliable form of theology: the true theologian *saw* and *experienced* the content of his theology, which was inseparable from contemplation. At the same time as our mystics were writing in England, this principle became definitive in the Greek Christian empire of Byzantium. Greek theologians who had been trained in Italy and who had been very impressed by Aquinas and his Aristotelian Christianity were opposed and defeated by St. Gregory Palamas, who refused to consider God in any sense as a concept, however inspiring, that could be rationally discussed and analyzed.

We know nothing at all about the author of *The Cloud of Unknowing.* He concealed his identity with such success that we may guess that his desire to remain hidden was probably deliberate. We do not know, therefore, whether he had himself been repelled by an arid scholastic theology that so frequently reduced "God" to an idea that our limited minds could grasp. He seems to have been more attuned to Greek than to Latin spirituality, however. The mystical writings of the fifth-century author who had adopted the pseudonym Dionysius the Areopagite were quite well known in Europe, even though they never had the same appeal for Europeans as they had for the Greeks. Our author, however, also seems to have translated Dionysius's *Mystical Theology* into English. In *The Cloud of Unknowing* he did not present the whole complexity of the Greek mystic's vision, but dwelt upon his central belief that God is ultimately and essentially incomprehensible to the human mind and that if we want to "know" God in this life, we must divest ourselves of all our ideas about the reality that we call "God." Jewish and Muslim mystics had also made the same radical claim. In the sixteenth century, St. John of the Cross would repeat that all human conceptions and preconceptions had to be left behind and that the soul must approach the utterly transcendent deity in a Dark Night.

Dionysius, like some of the earlier Greek fathers of the church, was inspired by the story of Moses' revelation on Mount Sinai. Moses had made the arduous climb to the top of the mountain, but on the summit he did not experience God himself but a thick cloud of unknowing.[1] He had come to the place where God was but had not encountered the ineffable reality itself. The Greeks pondered this image lovingly and urged Christians to realize that all our human ideas about God, no matter how inspiring or helpful they might seem to be, must be treated with the very greatest caution and cast aside if necessary. God, said Dionysius, is not only above our notions of goodness but he is above "God" himself as we understand him. Dionysius the Areopagite had adopted the name of St. Paul's first Greek convert. Since the earliest days of their conversion to Christianity, Greek Christians had been involved in a creative effort to baptize their glorious past and to wed it to the originally semitic Christian experience. Yet this meant that they also wanted to transcend the limitations of the Greek achievement in the light of the new faith. They were never as enthusiastic about ancient Greek rational philosophy as the Latin Western Church but felt its limitations acutely. The image of Moses enveloped in the cloud of unknowing seemed to express the kind of spirituality they were trying to create. This was not an ecstatic vision of God that laid aside human intelligence. It was an attempt to cultivate an attitude of mind that recognized that this intelligence — however glorious — had its limitations when it was confronted with the ineffable and ultimate reality. Hence their wariness of any human concepts about God that threatened to become a new idolatry that could be mistaken for the reality itself. Thus one might, said Dionysius, say that God was "good," but it was necessary to qualify this in the same breath: God was indeed good; he was Goodness itself, but he was not "good" in the limited way that human beings understood this quality. The Greeks found this agnostic approach yielded a sense of presence and bliss that transfigured their lives: it gave them the discipline to apprehend a reality infinitely greater than they could conceive, even though at the same time its absence was acutely felt.

This Greek venture shows the creative nature of the religious experience. It was obviously different from the religion of Jesus, as far as we understand it, and also from the Jewish vision of St. Paul, who had been the first to bring the Semitic faith to the Hellenistic world of the Roman Empire. Their negative theology was able to make the original revelation particularly their own and offered a constant corrective to their Hellenistic love of rationalism and intellectual debate. They took the Jewish scriptures as their starting point but evolved a unique and inspiring spirituality that spoke to their own condition. Their agnostic approach may prove to be more robust than the more rationalistic and positive vision evolved by the Christian West. It is not as vulnerable to logical and scientific attack, because, as the Greeks have always insisted, God is above and essentially opaque to, rational discussion. Russians adopted the orthodox spirituality of the Greeks and it is interesting that, even after decades of Soviet oppression, they do not have the same problems about the reality they call "God" as we do in the West, where Christians have always behaved as though God could be discussed like any other metaphysical entity.

The author of *The Cloud of Unknowing* had been able to

overcome a deep historical prejudice in his enthusiasm for Greek spirituality. By the fourteenth century relations between the Greek and Latin churches were at a nadir. The Latins had felt jealous of and hostile to their eastern Christian neighbor for centuries, and in 1204 the armies of the Fourth Crusade had sacked the Byzantine capital of Constantinople with horrible and immoral savagery; they may also have fatally weakened the Greek empire. The Greeks could not forgive this outrage, and when, during the fifteenth century, they repeatedly asked the West for help against the Ottoman Turks, the Latins were decidedly lukewarm in their response. The Roman Church had become very powerful and dismissed the Greeks as impious heretics who were not on the same level as the Holy Church of the West. But, unlike most of his contemporaries, the author of *The Cloud of Unknowing* felt that the Greek experience of God had something to offer the Christians of Western Europe. His is an example that we should, perhaps, consider carefully in our own day, when occasionally an inherited prejudice or imagined superiority makes us dismiss the religions of people who have followed other venerable and inspiring forms of faith that could revitalize our own tradition.

The *Cloud of Unknowing* is a monograph. The author makes no attempt to form a comprehensive view of the spiritual life, as Walter Hilton would attempt in *The Ladder of Perfection*. He is quite frank about this. He acknowledges that before a contemplative is ready, like Moses, to climb the mountain, he must prepare himself by the time-honored Western disciplines of *Lectio, Meditatio,* and *Oratio* — study of scripture, meditation, and prayer — but he tells his readers that other authors will tell them all they need to know about this. Instead he seeks to expound the agnostic attitude, which refuses to consider concepts or ideas about God — however inspiring and beneficial — in place of the ineffable reality of

God himself and tries to interpret traditional Christian beliefs and morality in the light of this mystical discipline.

He is aware that many Christians of his day — as in our own — find the whole idea of the contemplative life alien. What is the good of people who shut themselves away from their fellow men? He realizes it is probably impossible for the people he calls "actives" and "contemplatives" to understand one another. Both do what their temperaments and the grace of God dictate: neither can live their religious lives in any other way. We have seen that the ubiquity of the mystical compulsion has made most religions cultivate a contemplative strain, even when this seems alien to the original spirit of the founder. Our author is aware of these objections but, even though Christ plays little part in his religious vision, he does find a contemplative exemplar in the gospels in the story of Martha and Mary. It was common for Western Christians of the Middle Ages to see these two friends of Jesus as the first exponents of the active and contemplative life, respectively. Walter Hilton also refers to this story:

> In the course of his journey [Jesus] came to a village, and a woman named Martha welcomed him into her house. She had a sister called Mary, who sat down at the Lord's feet and listened to him speaking. Now Martha who was distracted with all the serving said, "Lord, do you not care that my sister is leaving me to do all the serving by myself? Please tell her to help me." But the Lord answered: "Martha, Martha," he said, "you worry and fret about so many things, and yet few are needed, indeed only one. It is Mary who has chosen the better part; it is not to be taken from her."[2]

Like many readers before and since, the author of *The Cloud of Unknowing* identified Mary the contemplative with Mary Magdalene and with the woman who had anointed the feet of

Christ, washed them with her tears, and who was told by Jesus that her sins had been forgiven because of her great love.

The Cloud of Unknowing suggests that Mary gazed through the humanity of Christ and glimpsed his divinity, albeit in a veiled and incomplete form. The Greeks preferred to find their gospel example of the contemplative life in the story of the Transfiguration of Jesus on Mount Tabor, when his glory shone through his humanity and his garments became as white as snow to the astonishment and joy of three of his disciples who were privileged to see this vision.[3] In their original context both stories had a different significance, but it was as impossible for fourteenth-century Christians to experience the Christian revelation in the same way as the first Christians as it is for us today. The history of religion demands a constant imaginative and creative effort to plumb the sources for new insight to meet the demands and needs of the present. Both Greeks and Latins had transformed the original Christian message to meet their own condition, and both needed to develop a contemplative tradition within this active faith when the time was right.

The author begs his readers not to be too hard on contemplatives: their lives are not useless. Many people in the late twentieth century also feel that the contemplative life seems self-indulgent and unproductive, but in fact, as we see in Walter Hilton's work, solitaries, hermits, and contemplative monks and nuns did not withdraw completely from the world. People felt free to consult them about all kinds of social, political, spiritual, and psychological problems. Somebody like Julian of Norwich was always in her cell and was therefore always available for people who needed help. Contemplatives often acted as medieval social workers or therapists and because they cultivated a receptive attitude of quiet openness to God they were probably excellent listeners. Certainly many

enclosed monks and nuns today are famous for their wise —
and frequently surprisingly worldly — advice. The author of
The Cloud of Unknowing, however does not discuss this social
dimension of the contemplative vocation in his monograph:
that is one of the things that he leaves to other writers.

Readers should not be repelled by the author's oft-
repeated advice to "trample" on the intellect and imagination.
He just as frequently admits that our ideas and imaginings can
be extremely useful in our quest for God. But yet again we
must remember that he is writing a monograph and describing one contemplative discipline where intellect and imagination have no place. The practice he proposes is a corrective to
the rather dogmatic habit that religious people often have of
saying that God wills this, forbids that, or dislikes the other, as
though God were a personality with likes and aversions similar to our own. All too frequently we can assume that our
ideas about God or the way we imagine "him" actually corre-
sponds to the indescribable reality itself and this can lead to a
form of idolatry: the worship of human images of the divine.
Instead, the author invites us all to try to by-pass ideas and
imaginings from time to time. If nothing else, we will gain a
deeper appreciation of the ineffable mystery that we call
"God."

The author of *The Cloud of Unknowing* is aware that his
view of the Christian life is controversial. But he is never
arrogant, strident, or aggressive when he presents his case.
He is a born teacher who always keeps his pupil in mind,
gently leads him from point to point, and is always ready to
anticipate his next question or objection. In particular, he
urges his disciple not to become anxious about his failures and
not to strain himself in his quest for perfection. Perhaps the
most moving sentence in the whole book comes in the last
chapter as he takes his leave of his reader: "For it is not what
you are nor what you have been that God regards with his

most merciful eyes, but what you would like to be." The spirituality of *The Cloud of Unknowing* never became as popular in the West as the *Mystical Theology* of Dionysius has remained in eastern Orthodox Christianity, but perhaps in our own day when many people in the Western world have reacted against inadequate human ideas of God, this book might prove to be a refreshing and useful corrective.

The Cloud of Unknowing

Chapter 1: My Friend in God

My spiritual friend in God, in my clumsy way I have found that there are four ways of living the Christian life: Common, Special, Solitary, and Perfect. The first three begin and end in this life, while the fourth may start here but it lasts forever in the joy of heaven. You will notice, moreover, that I have listed them in a certain order: first the Common or normal Christian life, then the Special or religious life, next the Solitary life and, finally, the Perfect life in God. It seems to me that, in his great mercy, our Lord has called you and drawn you toward him through the desire of your own heart in exactly the same order.

Thus you know very well that while you were living the Common life with your friends in the world, God's eternal love (through which he created and fashioned you and then redeemed you with the price of his precious blood when you were lost in Adam) would not let you remain so far away from him in that way of life. So he very kindly kindled your longing for him and bound you to him on a chain of desire and thus led you into a more Special state to live with his

familiar servants. There you could learn to live in his service more spiritually and enjoy a greater intimacy with him
than you had been able to do before in the world. And then
what?

It seems that he was still not content to leave you just
there because of the love that he has had for you since the first
moment of your existence. So what did he do? Don't you see
how lovingly and graciously he has drawn you apart into his
own intimate circle, into the third or Solitary way of life?
There you could learn to take your first steps into the way of
Perfection, the highest state of all.

Chapter 2: The Contemplative Vocation

Now, you feeble wretch, pause and take a look at yourself. Who do you think you are and what have you done to
deserve this summons from our Lord? How contemptible and
lazy is that heart which fails to respond to the profound
attraction of God's loving call! At this stage, poor creature
that you are, you must beware of the enemy. Never let the
dignity of your calling to the solitary life make you consider
yourself holier or better than other people; indeed, you will be
more despicable and worthy of blame if you do not do your
very best to live up to your vocation, with the help of God's
grace and by seeking expert advice. You should be all the
more humble and loving to your spiritual bridegroom because
he who is almighty God, King of Kings, and Lord of Lords has
desired to bring himself humbly down to your level and has
chosen you out of all his flock to be one of his particular
companions, setting you in a pasture where you can be fed
with the sweetness of his love, as a pledge of your eternal
inheritance in the kingdom of heaven.

So press on, I beg you, and hold to your purpose. Look

ahead of you, not back, and keep your eyes fixed on what you lack rather than on what you have because that is the surest way of gaining and preserving humility. If you are going to achieve perfection, your whole life must be filled with a yearning that must be planted in the depths of your being by almighty God himself, with your consent. But I must warn you of one thing: he is a jealous lover; he will not share your heart with anybody and will only work in your heart and will if he is in sole possession. He asks help of no one but yourself. All he wants you to do is to keep your gaze fixed on him and to let him do the rest. Keep the windows and the doors of your heart locked against the assaults of the enemy. And if you are ready to do this, you need only lean on God humbly in prayer and he will soon come to your rescue. Lean on him, then, and see how he bears your weight. He is absolutely ready and is only waiting for you. But what do you have to do? What does it mean to "lean upon him"?

Chapter 3: The Cloud of Unknowing

Lift up your heart to God in a humble impulse of love and aim for him alone, not for any of the good things you want from him. Try, indeed, to hate thinking about anything but him, so that there is nothing at work in your mind or heart but only him. You should, moreover, do everything you can to forget all the things that God has ever created and all the things that they, in their turn, have brought about, so that none of your thoughts or longings are directed to or harking after any single one of them, in general or particular. Leave them alone and take no notice of them. This is the work of the soul that pleases God most. All the saints and angels take great joy in this work and hasten to encourage it all they can. All the demons are furious when you engage in this activity and they will try to frustrate it by every method in their power. All the people living in the world are wonderfully helped by this work in ways that you cannot imagine. Yes, the power of this work even brings the souls in purgatory some relief from their pain. You yourself are purified and become more strong in virtue by means of this work than by any other. And yet no work is easier or achieved more quickly, provided that a soul is helped on by grace and has a conscious longing for it. Otherwise it is difficult and beyond your capacity.

Don't stop, therefore, but apply yourself to it assiduously until you feel this longing. When you first begin you only encounter a darkness and, as it were, a cloud of unknowing. You don't know what is happening, except that you feel that your will is starkly and strenuously bent upon God. Whatever you do, the darkness and cloud come between you and your God and prevent you from seeing him clearly by the light of intelligence and reason, nor can you experience him emotionally in the sweet consolations of love. So prepare yourself to wait in this darkness for as long as you can, yearning all the time for him whom you love. For if you are going to experience or see God in this life it can only be in this cloud and in this darkness. And if you really intend to work hard, as I advise you, I have faith that, through his mercy, you will achieve this state.

From Chapter 4: We Cannot Know God with the Intellect

I must tell you a little more about this matter, as I see it, in case you make some mistake and get the wrong idea about contemplation.

This work doesn't take a long time, as some people think. Indeed, it is the quickest work imaginable: it is never any longer or shorter than an atom, which, astronomers tell us, is the smallest unit of time, so tiny that it cannot be divided up and its brevity almost eludes our understanding. This is the time of which it is written: "You will have to give an account of all the time that has been given to you." And this demand is quite reasonable, because it is no longer or shorter than a single act of your will, which is the most important part of your soul. For there are just as many intentions or longings made by your will in an hour as there are atoms in that space of time. And if grace could refashion you to the state of man before the Fall, you would, by the help of that grace, always be able to control each one of those impulses, so that not a single one would slip by but they would all be directed to the chief object of desire and the pinnacle of all the things we will, which is God.

For God limits his divinity to come down to our level and our souls find an affinity with him because we have the great distinction of having been created in his image and likeness. And he alone and only he is able to fulfill the longing and intentions of our soul; by virtue of his grace, which re-creates us, our soul is capable of comprehending him completely by love, though God can never be comprehended by any created intelligence — either by a human being or by an angel. But by that I mean that they do not comprehend him in their understanding, not by means of their love. He is only incomprehensible to their intelligence, not to their love.

Every single rational creature has two faculties: the power of knowledge and the power of love. God is always quite unable to be comprehended by the first faculty, that of intelligence, but he is totally and perfectly comprehensible by the second, the power of love. Every single creature, moreover, will know him differently. Thus, each loving soul on its own can, through love, know him who is wholly and incomparably more than sufficient to fulfill all human souls or angels that could possibly exist. And this is the eternal and extraordinary miracle of love, because God will continue in this activity forever, without ceasing. Dwell on this, if you have the grace to do so, because to experience this for oneself is everlasting joy, and the contrary is everlasting pain. . . .

So pay attention to his wonderful divine activity in your soul. Properly understood, it is always an impromptu and unpremeditated impulse, which leaps up to God as a spark springs from the coal. The number of such impulses that can be achieved in the space of a single hour by a soul that is inclined to this work is extraordinary. In just one of these impulses he could have completely forgotten the whole created world. Yet because we are fallen creatures, he can quickly fall prey after each impulse to some thought or memory of some deed that he has either done or left undone. But so what? The soul can immediately spring up again as unexpectedly as it did before.

This is the correct way to understand this work. And you should be quite clear that we are not talking about fantasy or a disordered imagination or any obscure and esoteric belief. Those works are the product of a proud and inquisitive mind that enjoys imagining things that do not exist, not of a humble stirring of love and blind faith. That kind of conceited and ingenious mental activity must be stamped out ruthlessly and trodden underfoot if this work of grace is to be properly understood and performed with a pure intention.

For anyone who reads or hears about this work and imagines that it can be achieved by intellectual effort and so sits down and tries to work it out cerebrally is barking up the wrong tree. He is concocting an experience that is neither physical nor spiritual and, however learned he may be, he has embarked on an extremely dangerous course. So much so, that if God does not mercifully intervene with some miracle to make him abandon this activity and acquire the humility to seek the advice of experienced contemplatives, he is likely to become seriously disturbed or else fall into the evil state of serious and demonic sins of the spirit. Thus, he could easily be lost for all eternity, body and soul.

So for the love of God be careful and don't put any great strain on your mind or imagination. For I tell you truthfully, you cannot achieve it by any such strain, so leave your intellectual and your imaginative skills strictly alone.

And don't imagine that because I refer to a "cloud" or "darkness" that I am talking about a cloud of vapors that evaporates into thin air or a darkness you see in your house when your candle has been extinguished. That is the kind of darkness you can imagine with some degree of mental ingenuity on the brightest summer's day, just as on the darkest winter's night you can imagine a bright shining light. Do not waste your time with any of these false ideas. I didn't mean anything like that. When I use the word "darkness" I mean an absence of knowledge, as when you say that the things you don't know or have forgotten are "dark" to you because you cannot see them with your inner eye. And for the same reason, this "cloud" is no cloud in the sky but a "cloud of unknowing" between you and your God.

Chapter 5: The Cloud of Forgetting

If you are ever going to arrive at this cloud and live and work in it as I direct you, then just as this cloud of unknowing is, as it were, above you and between you and your God, so you must put a cloud of forgetting between you and everything that God has made. Perhaps it may seem that you are very far away from God because of the cloud of unknowing between you, but surely it is more accurate to say that unless you have interposed this cloud of forgetting between you and the whole of God's creation, you are even further away from him. Now, whenever I mention "the whole created world" I do not simply mean the things and people created by God but also all the things that *they* have created in their turn and everything connected with each one of them. I make no exception for any single creature, physical or spiritual, and I won't exclude any one of their characteristics or effects, good or bad. All, in a word, must be hidden under the cloud of forgetting during contemplation.

But though it can sometimes be extremely helpful to think about a particular person or a thing that God has made and to consider what they are like or what they do, in this particular work this will be practically useless. Why? Because whenever we remember or think about any of God's creatures or their effects, a kind of spiritual light is kindled within us. The eye of your soul turns upon it and can even concentrate upon it, just as a marksman concentrates on his target. And I will tell you this: whatever you think about is, as it were, above you for the duration and comes between you and your God, so that as long as there is anything at all in your mind except God, you are that much further away from him.

Yes, I really mean it! Indeed, if I can say this without giving offense, in this type of contemplation it will be almost useless to think about the kindness or the greatness of God, or about our Lady or the saints and angels in heaven, or even to dwell upon the joys of heaven, if you should think, by such meditation, that you would thereby strengthen your determination. Because although it is a good thing to meditate on God's mercy and to love and praise him for it, it is still far better to dwell on the stark reality of God and to love him and praise him for himself and not for the things he has done.

Chapter 6: What Is God?

But now you are going to ask me: "How am I supposed to think about God himself? What is he?" and I can only answer: "I have no idea!"

Because with this question you have brought me into the darkness and the cloud of unknowing that I want you to be in yourself. For, through grace, a man can have perfect knowledge of everything else and can think adequately about other matters — even about the works of God himself — but nobody can think about God's essential being. So I must be willing to leave all the things I can conceive with my mind on one side and choose for my love the one thing that I cannot think about. Why? Because he can be loved most satisfactorily but he cannot be thought about. He can be grasped and held by love but never by thought. And that is why, although it can sometimes be beneficial to think carefully about the kindness and excellence of God and although this can be both a revelation and a part of contemplation, nevertheless in this work it must be thrown aside and covered with a cloud of forgetting. And you must step over it resolutely and gladly and with a dedicated and pleasurable impulse of love try to pierce the darkness that you seem to encounter above you. And beat upon that thick cloud of unknowing with a sharp dart of yearning love. And never for a second think of giving up.

Chapter 7: Trample on Your Thoughts!

If a thought rises to the surface of your mind and persistently interposes itself between you and that darkness, demanding of you: "What are you looking for and what do you want?" you must answer that it is God that you want, saying, "It is he whom I long for, he I am looking for and nothing but God himself will do!"

And if this mental irritation goes on asking you: "What is God?" you must reply that God is the being who made you, who redeemed you, and who graciously called you to the religious life and then retort: "And you have absolutely no capacity for him whatever!" Then go on to say to this intellectual activity: "Down with you!" and trample on him out of a blind love of God, even if it seems a very holy thought that can only help you to seek God. The intellect may introduce beautiful and wonderful ideas into your mind about God's mercy, pointing out that he is the epitome of sweetness, love, grace, and kindness. And he will be delighted if you will entertain these thoughts, because he will go on chattering more and more till he pulls you down to consider Christ's Passion.

And then the intellect will impress upon you the miraculous kindness of God, and, again, he wants nothing more than to get you to listen to him. Because soon he will bring your old hopeless way of life to your attention and perhaps while you are considering your past wretchedness, he will bring to mind a place you used to live in. And so finally, before you know it, your mind will be completely distracted and scattered all over the place. The reason why you became distracted was that at first you listened willingly to the part of your mind that forms concepts, then you responded to it, entertained it, and let it take you over.

And yet it is still true that the idea suggested by your mind was both good and holy. Indeed, it was so holy that any man or woman who thinks that they will take up contemplation without having prepared themselves with many such reflective meditations on their own helplessness, the Passion of Christ, the mercy, goodness, and sublime excellence of God, is bound to fail or make some serious mistakes. But still, a man or a woman who has spent a long time on such reflections must leave them behind, cast them aside and suppress them under a cloud of forgetting, if he is ever going to pierce the cloud of unknowing between him and God. So when you decide to begin this work and feel that you have been called, by a special favor of God, to contemplation, lift up your heart to God with a humble stirring of love. And aim for God, who created you, redeemed you, and has given you the grace of a vocation to the religious life, and don't admit a single thought *about* God. It depends on you; you might not even want to remember our creation, redemption, and the rest. It is enough to have a naked intention directed to God and God alone without any other meditation.

You can, if you like, encapsulate and contain this intention in a single word, to help you concentrate. So take a little word of just one syllable to help you focus your attention. The shorter the word the better, because it is more like this particular activity of the Holy Spirit. Choose a word like "God" or "love" or any other word of one syllable that appeals to you and impress it indelibly on your heart so that it is always there, whatever happens.

This word must be your shield and your spear in times of peace or war alike. With this word you must batter the cloud and the darkness above you. With this word you must beat down all kinds of intellectual or analytical activity under the cloud of forgetting. So much so that if you are ever tempted to ask what you are looking for, answer with this one word — don't try to find other words or concepts. And if you should be tempted to analyze and reflect learnedly on the meaning of this word, your talisman, insist that you want to preserve it as a simple whole and not divide and subdivide it into separate categories. If you are determined to hold fast to your purpose, you can be confident that thought will eventually fade away. Why? Simply because you will not let your mind feed on the consoling meditations about God that we mentioned earlier.

Chapter 8: The Active and the Contemplative

But now you are bound to ask me whether this constant temptation to have ideas is good or bad. "If it really is an evil impulse," you will argue, "then I am surprised that it increases a man's devotion so much. Sometimes it seems extremely consoling to listen to my thoughts, which can, for example, reduce me to tears of empathy when I meditate on the Passion of Christ or my own sinfulness, and it inspires me to other ideas that seem to me to be holy and to have done me a great deal of good. So it seems that thinking simply cannot be dismissed as evil; and if it is a good thing and if consoling ideas can be so helpful, then I confess that I am amazed that you should tell me to repress them so thoroughly under the cloud of forgetting."

Now I agree that this is a very good point, so I am going to try to answer it to the best of my poor ability. First, when you ask me what it is that interrupts your contemplation so insistently, I reply that it is a precise and distinct perception of your natural intelligence; it proceeds from the reasoning part of the soul. And if you ask me whether it is good or bad, I reply that in itself it must essentially be good because our reason is a reflection of God's own mind. But we can use our intellect for good and evil ends. When we open our minds to God's grace and consider our sinfulness, the Passion, God's mercy and his wondrous work in his creation, physical and spiritual, this activity is good. No wonder it increases your devotion as much as you say! But reason can be evil when it is inflated with egotistic pride and by a shallow curiosity for abstruse knowledge and a lust for intellectual ingenuity. Look how some of the clergy abuse their minds! Their reason does not make them ambitious to be revered as humble scholars and students of the divine word and for their piety. They want to be scholars of the devil and students of vanity and falsehood. So too with other men and women, whatever their vocation, religious or secular: the activity of their natural intelligence is evil when it is swollen with pride, inspired by a barren subtlety in worldly matters, and wastes itself in unspiritual casuistry as part of a quest for honor and glory in this world, and when they desire to obtain material rewards, empty pleasures, and flattery.

If you were to ask me why you have to suppress this capacity for thought under a cloud of forgetting, even though it is a good thing in itself and can be extremely helpful and increase your devotion to God, provided it is used properly, this would be my answer: You have to realize that there are two ways of life in Holy Church. One is the active life and the other is the contemplative life. In the active life there are ranks, a higher and a lower, and likewise the contemplative life has a higher and a lower rank. These two ways of life are linked, despite their differences from one another. They are interdependent and you cannot live one of them without participating in some way in the other. Why is this? Because the higher rank of the active life is the lower part of the contemplative life. This means that no one can lead a fully active life without being partly contemplative, nor can anybody be wholly contemplative (at least in this life) unless he is partly active. The active life belongs essentially to this world: it begins and ends there. But this is not true of the contemplative life, which starts in this world but continues into eternity. Why? The part that Mary chose, as Scripture says, will never be taken away from her. The active life is busy and troubled about many things, but the contemplative sits in peace with the one thing necessary.

The lower part of the active life consists of good, plain acts of mercy and charity. The higher part of the active life and the lower part of the contemplative consists of excellent spiritual meditations and also of ceaseless consideration of our

particular sins to induce sorrow and remorse as well as
thoughts of the Passion of Christ and of his saints to induce a
spirit of compassion and also of the marvelous gifts of God —
his kindness to all the things he has made, spiritual and
physical — to encourage a spirit of praise and thanksgiving.
But the higher part of the contemplative life, insofar as it is
possible to live it here on earth, is entirely dependent on the
darkness and the cloud of unknowing that I have mentioned;
it consists simply of a reaching out in love in a blind concen-
tration on the naked reality of God as he is in himself and on
him alone.

In the lower part of the active life, all the activities that a
man engages in are outside himself and, as it were, beneath
him. In the higher part of the active life (which, of course, is
also the lower part of the contemplative life), a man lives
within himself and on his own level, as we might say. But in
the higher part of the contemplative life, a man is reaching
above his own nature and is only subordinate to God. He is
living above himself because he is trying, through grace, for a
state that he cannot achieve by natural means, that is, to be
united spiritually to God and to be one with him in love and
the surrender of his will. So, just as nobody can achieve the
higher state of the active life unless he refrains for a time from
his acts of charity in the lower degree, it is impossible for
anybody to reach the higher part of the contemplative life
unless he refrains from practicing the duties of a lower stage.

You see, it would be quite improper and destructive for a
man who was engaged in meditation to think about his exterior works of mercy at that time or to turn his mind to
consider all he had been doing and all that remained to be
done, even though these charitable deeds were in themselves
extremely holy. So surely it would be equally damaging and
improper when a man was at work in the darkness and in the
cloud of unknowing and was eagerly reaching out in love to

God as he is in himself, if he allowed any thoughts or meditation on God's marvelous gifts and his kindness to all his creatures, physical and spiritual, to rise up in his mind and come between him and God, even though in themselves they were extremely holy, profound, and consoling.

This is why I insist that you suppress any interesting or clever ideas in the cloud of forgetting, however holy or promising they seem, even if they would appear to help you in your contemplation. Because it is love and not knowledge that will enable us to reach God in this life. All the time we are living in this mortal body, the clarity of our perception of spiritual matters is always distorted by some kind of illusion, and this applies particularly to our ideas about God. This inevitably spoils our contemplation, and it would be surprising if it did not lead us into serious error.

Chapter 9: Suppress the Imagination

And so it is important to suppress the energetic activity of your intellect, which always tries to overwhelm you whenever you settle down to contemplation, because unless you keep it under control, it will suppress you! So often when you are imagining that you are really immersed in this darkness and that there is nothing in your mind but God, if you really examine yourself you will find that instead of inhabiting the darkness your mind is busily occupied with something less than God. And when that happens you can be sure that this lesser object of contemplation overshadows you while you are engaged with it and comes between you and your God. Therefore you must make the decision to repress all inspiring reflections, no matter how holy or promising they seem. Because I will tell you one thing: this blind groping for God as he is in himself and this intimate pressing upon the cloud of unknowing is more conducive to your spiritual health, more valuable in itself, and more pleasing to God and to all the angels and saints in heaven — not to mention its being more helpful to your friends on the natural and spiritual levels, whether they are alive or dead — than any kind of meditation. It is better for you to cultivate this and make it your chief spiritual enthusiasm than to reflect upon all the saints and angels in heaven or to contemplate the harmony and bliss that they enjoy for all eternity.

Don't be surprised by this. You would be of one mind with me if you had a clear perception of it just once and, indeed, by means of grace you can learn to struggle toward it and experience it in this life. But remember that you will never have an unclouded vision of God here below; you can only have an apprehension of him, through grace and when God allows it. So direct your love to that cloud, and with the help of his grace strive to forget everything else.

Indeed, if the mere recollection of anything less than God that surfaces in your mind involuntarily puts you at a greater distance from God than you would be otherwise, holding you back and making it more difficult for you to experience this love, then just think how harmful a thought that you have consciously and voluntarily cultivated will be! And if thoughts about a particular saint or about a purely spiritual matter will hold you back from God, then think how damaging thoughts of mere men living in this world or physical and worldly matters will be to you and your contemplation!

I am not saying that any spontaneous idea that rises in your mind against your will and conscious intention about a pure spiritual matter that is less than God, even if you cultivate it to increase your devotion, is actually evil, even though it will impede your progress in this kind of contemplation. No indeed! God forbid that you should misunderstand me in this way! But I do say that as long as you are engaged in this higher spiritual activity — however good or holy such a thought may be, it will be more of a hindrance than a help. Surely anybody who is wholly set on the quest for God can find no rest in the thought of a mere angel or saint in heaven.

Chapter 12: Virtue

If you want to stand fast in virtue and not fall prey to temptation, never let your intention fail. Beat constantly against the cloud of unknowing between you and your God with a piercing dart of longing love and be loath to let your mind wander on anything less than God. Don't give up for anything, because this is absolutely the only work that destroys the ground and root of sin. It doesn't matter how much you fast or keep long vigils, how early you get up, how hard your bed is, or how painful your hair shirt. Indeed, if it was lawful for you — as, of course, it isn't! — to pluck out your eyes, cut your tongue from your mouth, stop your ears and nose, lop off your limbs, and inflict all the pain that is possible or that you can imagine on your body, none of this would do you any good at all. The impulse and the temptation to sin would still be embedded in you.

What else can I tell you? However much you weep with remorse for your sins or sorrow for Christ's Passion or however firmly you fix your mind on the joys of heaven, what benefit would you derive? Certainly it would give you much good, much help, much profit, much grace. But compared with this blind yearning of love, it can do very little. This is the "best part" that Mary chose. Those who don't practice it make very little progress. Not only does it destroy the ground and root of sin, but it also builds the virtues. For if this loving impulse is properly rooted in the soul, it contains all the virtues, truly, perfectly, and effectually, without in any way diluting the intention of the will toward God. Indeed, it doesn't matter how many virtues a man acquires; without this true love they are bound to be warped and thus imperfect.

This is because virtue is nothing else but a properly ordered and deliberate turning of the soul to God. Why? God as he is in himself is the one and only source of all the virtues, so much so that if anyone is inspired to acquire a single virtue with mixed motives, even if God is uppermost in his mind, that virtue is bound to be flawed. We shall understand this better if we concentrate on just one or two particular virtues, and these may as well be humility and love. For anyone who has acquired these two virtues doesn't need any more: he has got them all.

Chapter 13: Humility

So let us first take a look at the virtue of humility, considering why it is flawed if it is inspired by any other motive than God himself, even if he is the chief cause; and we shall also consider why it is perfect if it is inspired by God himself. To start with, it is necessary to see in what humility essentially consists if we are going to understand it correctly. Then we can grasp more truly and in a spiritual way what its cause is.

Humility is essentially just a true knowledge and appreciation of ourselves, as we really are. It must be obvious that anyone who can really see and experience himself as he is is bound to be humble. There are two reasons for this humility: one is the filth, misery, and wretchedness into which man has fallen because of sin, and which he will always experience in this life to some extent, however holy he is. The other reason is the excessive love and excellence of God himself: gazing at this the whole natural world quakes in dread, scholars become idiots, and angels and saints blind. So much is this the case that if God, in his wisdom, did not temper their vision of his divinity to the level of their natural and God-given capacity, I daren't tell you what might happen to them.

The second cause is the perfect motive for humility, for the simple reason that it will last forever. The first motive is flawed not only because it will cease to exist at the end of this life but because it can very often happen that a soul in this mortal body can — because of God's abundant grace and his own increasing desire for as long as God deigns to inspire it — suddenly and completely lose all consciousness of himself and will not worry whether he is holy or sinful. But whether this happens often or very seldom to a soul that is so disposed, I believe that it only lasts a very short time. During this period, the soul is perfectly humble because it is inspired only by the chief motive of humility, which is God himself. As long as a soul experiences the other motive, even if the perfect motive remains predominant, his will be an imperfect humility. But for all that, this flawed humility is still good and we must strive to acquire it. God forbid that you should misunderstand me in this matter!

Chapter 16: The Story of Mary, Whom Christ
Forgave Because She Loved Much

Nobody, even if he is the most miserable sinner in the world, should think it presumptuous to offer up this humble impulse of love to God and to press inwardly against the cloud of unknowing between him and the Deity, once he has duly amended his life and has felt inspired to take up the contemplative life with the approval of his spiritual director and his own conscience. When our Lord said to Mary, who stood for all the sinners who are called to contemplation: "Your sins are forgiven you," it was not because of her great sorrow, nor for her meditations on her sins, and not even for her humility when she thought about her sins. So why was it? Surely, because she loved much.

Look! here we have an example of how much more an interior motion of love can gain from our Lord than any other activity that men can imagine. Yet I grant you, she was full of remorse and wept over her sins, and that the memory of her weakness made her very humble. So, too, those of us who have been miserable and habitual sinners should be filled with horror, astonishment, and sorrow for the rest of our lives and should be greatly humbled by the memory of our sinfulness.

But how should we do this? Surely, as Mary did. Even though she could not always *feel* a profound and heartfelt sorrow for her sins, yet she carried them with her all her life, like a huge weight in the depths of her heart so that she could not forget them. But Scripture tells us that she had a more heartfelt sorrow, a more grievous longing, and that she almost died of remorse because she did not love God enough. Although her heart was full of love, this longing to love was more pronounced than the memory of her sins. And we should not find this surprising, because it is the nature of a true lover that the more he loves the more he longs to love.

Yet she was very much aware in her own mind and felt a deep-rooted sadness that she was the most evil of all sinners and that her sins had separated her from the God she loved so much. She also knew that her sins were a major cause of her weakness and of her failure to love God enough. So what did she do about it? Did she descend from the exalted heights of her desire to the depths of her sinful life? Did she rake through the filth and sewage of her sins, bringing them up, one by one, for close examination, inquiring into the circumstances of each one and weeping and grieving over it individually? Certainly not! Because God's grace had made it clear to her at a very deep level that she would never achieve her heart's desire like this. That way she was more likely to enter a life of constant sin once more rather than to gain a straightforward forgiveness of all those sins.

So she pinned all her love and longing onto the cloud of unknowing and taught herself to love what she would never clearly understand by the light of her reason here below, nor would she feel the sweetness of her love emotionally. She was so successful in this that she sometimes forgot that she had been a sinner before. Yes, and very often I believe that she was so fully occupied in loving God as he is in himself that she paid little attention to the beauty of Christ's physical body when he sat before her, speaking and teaching. Nor did she notice anything else, physical or spiritual. This is what the gospel seems to tell us.

Chapter 17: Mary and Martha

In St. Luke's gospel it is written that when our Lord was in Martha's house, her sister Mary sat at his feet while Martha was busy preparing his food. While Mary was listening to Jesus, she took no notice of her sister's activity, even though it was extremely good and holy and the first stage of the active life. Nor did she notice Jesus' precious body nor the sweetness of his voice and the humanity of his words, even though such meditation is even better and holier, being the second stage of the active life and the first stage of the contemplative life.

Indeed, Mary gazed with all the love in her heart at the sublime wisdom of Christ's divinity, which was hidden in the mysterious words of his humanity. Nothing that she saw or heard around her could make her stir; she sat as physically still as she could and with a secret, delightful, and yearning love she pressed against the vast cloud of unknowing between her and her God. I tell you, nobody, however pure, ever has been or ever will be so rapt in the contemplation and love of God in this life that he does not encounter this sublime and wondrous cloud of unknowing between him and God. It was against this cloud that Mary pressed with her interior acts of love. Why? Because it was the highest and holiest degree of contemplation that can be attained in this present life, so she refused to stop it. When, therefore, her sister Martha complained about her to our Lord and asked him to tell her sister to get up and help her and not to let her work so hard on her own, Mary sat as still as she could and did not say a word or even gesture impatiently at her sister, despite her complaints. No wonder; she was engaged in another kind of work that Martha knew nothing about, so she had no time to listen to her complaints or answer back.

Look, friend! All that happened between our Lord and these two sisters — their actions, words and gestures — serves as an example to all the actives and contemplatives who have lived in Holy Church since that time to the Day of Judgment. Mary stands for the contemplatives, who should all model their lives on her behavior, and Martha, for the same sort of reason, stands for the actives.

Chapter 18: Tension Between Actives and Contemplatives

Just as Martha lodged a complaint at that time against her sister, so, too, actives complain about contemplatives right up to the present day. Because as soon as a man or a woman belonging to a particular organization in this world, religious or secular — I make no exceptions — feel themselves inspired by grace or their spiritual advisers to abandon all their external duties to live a fully contemplative life, as their talents and conscience direct them, their brothers, sisters, and best friends together with many other people who understand nothing about this interior compulsion or this way of life are bound to rise against them, complaining irritably that they are not doing anything at all. And they will come up with stories of men and women who have taken up this way of life previously — some of the stories are true, some false — and failed. They never have a word to say about those who succeeded.

I grant you that many people who seem to have forsaken the world do fall by the wayside. Because they refused to follow prudent spiritual advice and instead of becoming God's servants and contemplatives, they became the servants and contemplatives of the devil. They fell in with hypocrites or heretics or else fell into delusions and other dangerous practices that are a scandal to the Church. I don't want to confuse the issue by discussing these people at the moment, but later on, if it is necessary and if it is God's will, we may look at their circumstances and the reason for their failure. So no more of them for the time being, but let us move on to the matter at hand.

Chapter 19: Actives Like Martha Are Usually Ignorant About the Contemplative Life

Now some people may think that I am showing too little respect for Martha, that special saint, in comparing her complaint against her sister to those worldly men's arguments, and vice versa. Truly, I mean no disrespect to her nor, for that matter, to these others. God forbid that I should say anything that could be interpreted as a condemnation of any of God's servants in any walk of life, never mind such a special saint! It seems to me that her complaint is excusable when we see it in the context of the time and the spirit in which she uttered it. Her ignorance prompted what she said. No wonder she didn't understand what Mary was doing at that time, because I am sure she had never heard of such a perfect way of life. She also spoke courteously and briefly, and so she must always be excused.

Likewise, it seems to me that those worldly men and women in the active life should also be fully exonerated for the complaints that I mentioned earlier. They may speak very rudely, but they are ignorant. Why? Because just as Martha had no idea of what Mary was up to when she complained about her to our Lord, so these folk nowadays know nothing or next to nothing about what God's disciples intend when they withdraw from worldly activity to become God's intimate servants in holiness and with a true spirit. If they really understood, I am sure that they wouldn't act or speak as they do, so we must excuse them. Why, they know no better way of life than their own, and moreover when I think about the countless mistakes I have made in the past due to my ignorance, then it seems to me that I must be restrained in my actions regarding their ignorance if I want God to forgive me my stupid misdeeds. Otherwise I would not be doing to others as I would want them to do to me.

Chapter 23: God Will Exonerate His Contemplatives

It is true that if we are zealous in our desire to model our love and lives on Mary, as far as we are able with the help of God's grace and with good spiritual advice, God will certainly answer for us every day in a secret, intimate way in the hearts of our detractors. I am not claiming that we shall never have our critics in this world, who will complain about us as they did about Mary. But I do say that if we take no more notice of their criticisms than she did and if we refuse to give up our interior spiritual work, then God will speak on our behalf in the hearts of our detractors, provided that they are sincere people, so that in a very few days they will feel ashamed of their thoughts and complaints.

Moreover, just as he justifies us spiritually in the souls of our critics, so too he will inspire other people to provide us with the things we need in this world — with food, clothing, and so on — once he sees that we won't leave off loving him to acquire them for ourselves. I am saying this to answer those who say that it is not right for people to serve God as contemplatives unless they have first provided for their physical needs. For, they say, the Lord helps those who help themselves. Indeed, they know very well that they are mistaken. For you can be quite certain, whoever you are, if you have really renounced the world for God, that he will give you one of these two things without your having to lift a finger: either he will give you more than you need or he will give you the physical strength and spiritual patience to suffer deprivation. So what does it matter which you have? It's all the same to true contemplatives. If anyone doubts this, then either the devil lives in his heart and has taken away his faith, or else he has not really turned to God as wholeheartedly as he should, however clever he seems or whatever pious justification he comes up with.

So you, who are trying to become a contemplative like Mary, have chosen to be made humble by the ineffable majesty and perfection of God — with perfect humility, therefore, rather than by considerations of your own sinfulness, which is imperfect humility. Make sure your gaze is fixed on the excellence of God rather than on your own frailty. For nothing shall be wanting to those who are perfectly humble, materially

or spiritually. Why not? Because they have God in Whom is
all abundance. Whoever has him — as this book keeps on
saying — doesn't need anything else in this life.

Chapter 24: Contemplation and the Virtue of Love

We have argued that humility is totally contained in this
blind, urgent love that beats against the dark cloud of unknowing and throws aside and forgets about everything else.
We can understand all the other virtues in the same way,
especially love. Because love is simply the love of God for
himself above all the things that he has made and to love men
for God's sake and as we love ourselves. And it seems quite
clear that in this work of contemplation, God is indeed loved
for himself above all creatures, for, as I said earlier, the essence of this work is nothing other than a single-minded
intention that is directed toward God as he is in himself.

I call it "single-minded" because in this work the perfect
apprentice doesn't ask to be spared pain or to receive a great
reward. He asks, to put it in a nutshell, only for God himself.
He is so intent on this that he neither cares nor notices
whether he is in pain or in ecstasy, as long as the will of him he
loves is fulfilled. It appears, therefore, that in this work God is
perfectly loved for himself and above all created things, because in this work a true practitioner cannot endure the mere
thought of the holiest thing in the world. We can also prove
that this work fulfills the second and lower branch of love,
which is directed toward our fellow Christians. Because in
this work, the true contemplative has no special interest in
anybody for their own qualities, whether he is a relation or a
stranger, a friend or an enemy. All men seem related to him
and nobody is a stranger; all are his friends and none is his
enemy. He will go so far as to say that all those who hurt and

damage him in this world are his special friends, and he seems inspired to seek their good as zealously as he would the good of his very best friend.

From Chapter 25: How a Contemplative Should Relate to Other People

When somebody is engaged in contemplation itself he will [not] have a special interest in anybody — friend or enemy, relative or stranger. That is impossible, because everything except God is completely forgotten when this work is properly done. This will make the contemplative so virtuous and charitable that when he does come down to earth and talks to or prays for his fellow Christians he can be as well-disposed to enemies as to friends, kin as to strangers. Indeed, he will sometimes incline more to his enemies than to friends! He should not, of course, ever give up contemplation entirely, because that is a great sin for a contemplative, but sometimes he has to come down for a while to respond to other people's needs, as charity demands.

But while he is occupied with his special work, he has no time to note who are friends and who are enemies, who kinfolk and who strangers. I am not saying that he won't sometimes — even quite often — feel more affectionate toward some people than others. That is perfectly all right, and charity demands this kind of love. Christ loved John, Mary, and Peter more than the others. But my argument is that while he is actually engaged in contemplation everybody is his friend because he must then experience God alone as the reason for loving, and everything must, therefore, be loved simply and purely for God's sake as well as their own.

Chapter 26: God Will Pierce the Cloud of Unknowing

Set to work, therefore, with all possible speed: beat against this high cloud of unknowing — you can rest later! It is extremely hard work for the beginner, make no mistake about that, unless God makes it easier with a special grace or simply because after a while one gets used to it.

But in what sense exactly is it hard work? Certainly not in the devout and urgent motion of love that is always springing up in the will of a contemplative, because this is not produced mechanically but by the hand of almighty God, who is always ready to act in each eager soul who has done and continues to do everything in his power to prepare himself for this work.

So why is it so arduous? Obviously in the trampling on all memory of God's creatures and keeping them enveloped by that cloud of forgetting I mentioned earlier. This really is hard work because *we* have to do it, with God's help; the other aspect of the work, which I have just described — the urgent impulse of love — is entirely the work of God. So do your part, and I promise you that he will not fail to do his.

Get to work as soon as possible, then. Let me see how you are bearing up. Can't you see that God is waiting for you? For shame! After just a short, hard period of effort you will find the immense difficulty of the work beginning to ease. It is true that it is hard and repressive at the start, when your devotion is weak, but later when you are more devout what once seemed extremely arduous has become much easier and you can begin to relax. You may only have to make a little effort — or even no effort at all, because sometimes God does everything himself. But this doesn't always happen, and never for very long, but whenever he chooses and as he chooses. But you will be more than happy then, so let him do what he likes.

At such a time, God may perhaps send out a beam of

spiritual light that pierces this cloud of unknowing between you and him and show you some of his secrets, of which mere men cannot speak. Then you will feel your affection kindled with the fire of his love in a way that I cannot describe to you. I cannot describe it to you at this time. For I dare not describe a work that belongs only to God with my blabbering, earth-bound tongue. Briefly, even if I dared, I would not. But I will gladly tell you about the work that a man must undertake, who is inspired and helped by grace. That is far less dangerous!

Chapter 27: Who Is Called to This Work?

First of all I will tell you who ought to practice this contemplation, when and how he should do it, and what are the conditions.

If you want to ask me who should engage in this work, I would reply: "Everybody who has really and with full deliberation abandoned the world not for the active life but for that kind of life that is called contemplative. Everybody who has received this vocation should undertake this work, with God's help, whoever they are, no matter whether they have been habitual sinners or not."

But if you ask me when they should start work, I would reply: "Not until they have purified their conscience of all the sins of their past life, according to the normal rules of Holy Church."

apter 31: Firmness with Distractions

once you feel that you have done everything you can
r life straight, according to the laws and judgment of

Holy Church, you must immediately put yourself to work. And then if you find that the memories of things you have done in your past life keep coming between you and your God or if a new idea or temptation distracts you, you must be firm and walk right over them, trampling them underfoot. Try to cover them with a thick cloud of forgetting, as though these things had never happened or occurred to you or anybody else. If they persist, then you must keep on stamping on them as often as they arise, and if this seems very difficult then there are special methods, techniques, and spiritual strategies that you can use to get rid of these distractions. These techniques are best learned from God by means of your own experience than from anybody else.

Chapter 32: Techniques to Get Rid of Distractions

I can, nevertheless, teach you something about these techniques, I think. By all means try them out and see if you can do better. Do everything in your power to behave as though you were unaware of these distractions, which keep thronging so urgently about you, getting between you and your God. Try to look over their shoulders, as it were, as though you were looking for something else: that "Something," of course, is God who is enclosed in the cloud of unknowing. If you do this, I think you will find that your toil quickly becomes easier. If this technique is properly understood, I believe that it is simply a yearning and a desire for God, a longing to experience and to see him as clearly as we can in this life. And this desire is charity, which will always make your task lighter.

Here is another technique for you to try if you wish. When you feel that there is no way that you can suppress these distractions, cower beneath them as though you were a

prisoner or a coward defeated in battle. Tell yourself that it is
pure stupidity to contend with them any longer: thus you will
give yourself up to God, while you are in the hands of your
enemies and feel that you have been permanently destroyed.
Please give this method your full consideration, because if you
try to put it into practice you are bound to fade away completely, and indeed it seems clear to me that if this technique is
properly understood it is simply an accurate understanding
and experience of yourself as you really are: a filthy wretch
who is worse than nothing. This experience and perception is
humility, which will always succeed in forcing God himself to
come down, as it were, to take revenge on your enemies, to
raise you up and to wipe the tears lovingly from the eyes of
your soul, just as a father does when his child is about to die in
the jaws of wild boars or mad, biting bears.

Chapter 35: Preliminary Disciplines for the Novice

But there are props that should be employed by the
apprentice in contemplation, namely *Lectio, Meditatio,* and *Oratio,* or, in terms that you will understand more easily, Reading,
Studying, and Praying. You can better learn about these
things in other books written by other authors, so I need not
go into detail here. But I will say this: these three exercises are
so closely linked that to beginners and to people who have
become proficient — though not to those who have reached
the Perfect state, as far as this is possible here below —
Studying is not possible unless it is preceded by Reading or
Listening. It is all one activity, whether we speak of the clergy
who read books or laypeople who, as it were, "read" when
they listen to priests preaching the word of God. Similarly,
beginners and those who have become proficient cannot Pray
unless they have started with Study.

We can test this out. God's word, whether it is written or spoken, can be compared to a mirror. Spiritually, reason is the eye of your soul and your conscience is your spiritual face. Just as it is impossible to see a dirty mark on your face without a mirror or somebody else who mentions it to you, so it is with the spiritual life: without Reading or listening to God's word it is impossible for the unaided reason of a habitual sinner to see a mark on his conscience.

We can take this one step further: when somebody sees a dirty mark in a mirror or when another person tells him where it is — this has a spiritual as well as a physical application — only then will he hurry to the well to wash it off. If this mark is a particular sin, then the well is the Church and the water the sacrament of Penance and all that goes with it. But if it is simply a deeply rooted evil habit, then the well is the God of mercy and the water is Prayer. So you can see that no meditation is possible for beginners or for experts unless they read or listen first; nor is prayer possible unless it is preceded by Study.

Chapter 36: The Prayer of One Syllable

But none of this applies to people who practice the type of contemplation described in this book, because their "meditations" are, so to speak, a sudden perception or an unanalytical awareness of their own sinfulness or of God's goodness, which come without any reading or listening beforehand and without any study of anything at all. You had better learn about these sudden perceptions and experiences from God himself rather than from other people. I don't mind if these days you undertake no meditation at all on the subject of your own sinfulness or God's goodness that cannot be summed up in the single word SIN or GOD or whatever word you like —

provided, that is, that you are inspired by God's grace and your spiritual director. You should not analyze or interpret these words cleverly in order to increase your devotion. In this work you should never do anything like that. Instead, keep the whole sense of these words in your mind, so that by SIN you mean a *lump:* you don't know what it is because in fact it is nothing but yourself. You would think that this experience of yourself as a sinful lump, with which you are completely identified, would make you crazier than anybody in the world, but nobody would guess this from looking at you: there you are, modest in your demeanor, making no strange faces, but whether you are sitting, walking, lying down, resting, standing, or kneeling you are always perfectly calm and relaxed!

Chapter 37: A Cry for Help

People who are trying to live the contemplative life find that their prayers, like their meditations, well up spontaneously. I am referring to their private prayers, you understand, not to the official prayers required by Holy Church: nobody values these prayers more than contemplatives, and they are careful to use the forms and rites laid down by the holy fathers before us. But their own personal prayers rise up to God without premeditation or any special direction, either before or during their devotions.

It is very rare for these kinds of prayers to take the form of words, but if they do they are very brief: the fewer words used, in fact, the better. Indeed, it's my opinion that a tiny word of one syllable is better than a word of two syllables and accords more perfectly to the work of the Holy Spirit, because a real contemplative should try to live continuously on a spiritual peak. This natural example shows us the truth

of the matter: a man or a woman who is suddenly frightened
by a fire or a death or something of this sort is in a state of
extremity and compelled to cry or pray at once for help.
How does he do this? Certainly you won't find him making a
long speech or even using a word of two syllables! Why?
Because it would take too long to express his need and
agitation. In his great terror, he bursts out with one little
monosyllable like "fire!" or "help!"

And just as that little word "fire!" catches people's attention more quickly, so does that little monosyllable that is
not spoken or even conceptualized but represents a secret
stirring in the depths of the soul. That is what I mean by the
"peak," because in the spiritual life height and depth, length
and breadth are all one and the same. This penetrates the
ears of almighty God more surely than some interminable
psalm mumbled mechanically, and that is why it is written
that a short prayer pierces heaven.

Chapter 38: The Power of a Short Prayer That Involves the Whole Person

So why does this tiny little prayer of one syllable pene-
trate the heavens? Surely because a person involves his whole
heart when he prays like this in the height, depth, length, and
breadth of his spirit. We can say that it is in the height,
because it requires all his spiritual power; in the depth, because this little syllable contains all spiritual knowledge; in the
length, because if the soul could continue to feel what it feels
now it would continually cry out in this way; in the breadth,
because it would extend to all mankind what it longs for itself.

It is at a moment like this that a soul grasps the lesson
taught by St. Paul and all the saints — perhaps not entirely but
to the extent that is possible at this stage of contemplation —

namely, the length, the breadth, the height, and the depth of the everlasting, all-loving, all-powerful, and all-knowing God. God's eternity is his "length"; his love is his "breadth," his power is his "height," and his wisdom is his "depth." It is no wonder that a soul who is transformed so closely into the image and likeness of God, his creator, is heard by God so quickly. Yes, even a very sinful soul, who is, as it were, God's enemy, who is enabled by grace to cry out this tiny syllable in the height and depth, the length and the breadth of his spirit, would always be heard and helped by God because of the fearful anguish of his cry.

Take this example. If you heard your deadly enemy so frightened that he cries out this little word "fire!" or "help!" in his extremity, the fact that he was your enemy wouldn't even cross your mind, but the sorrow in his cry would rouse such pity in your heart that you would not hesitate — even in the depths of winter — to help him extinguish the fire or soothe his distress. O Lord! if a mere man can lay his enmity aside by means of grace to show such pity and mercy, what pity and mercy must God feel when he hears the spiritual cry of a soul, uttered in the height, the depth, the length, and the breadth! God has by nature everything that man has by means of grace. And far more, incomparably more mercy must God show, because a quality that is essential to the nature of a thing brings it closer to eternity than a quality acquired by grace.

Chapter 39: What Is Prayer?

That is what it means, therefore, to pray in the height, the depth, the length, and the breadth of the spirit. It is not a prayer of many words, but a little word of one syllable. What should this word be? It will inevitably depend on the nature of prayer itself. What word is that? First, we have to consider what prayer really is and then we will be in a position to know the word that expresses the nature of prayer most perfectly.

In itself, prayer is simply a devout orientation to God himself to acquire good and remove evil. So, since all evil is comprised in the concept of sin, either in origin or essence, when we pray with the intention of removing evil, we should neither say, nor think, nor mean anything more elaborate than this little word "sin." And when we pray with the intention of acquiring good, then let us cry, in word, or thought, or desire, just this word "God" and nothing else, because all good is found in God, the origin and essence of goodness. Don't be surprised that I have chosen these words in preference to any others. If I could have found other words that comprised all goodness and all evil as perfectly as these two, I would certainly have used them and rejected "God" and "sin." So I advise you to do the same.

But don't analyze these words. If you attempt this, you will never become a contemplative, because no amount of study can teach you this kind of prayer but only grace. So, in spite of all that I have said, only use those words that God has inspired you to utter in prayer. But if God should inspire you to use these two, I advise you not to reject them, if you intend to use words at all in your prayer, that is. If not, don't bother with any words at all.

These are very short words; but even though the brevity of prayer is recommended here, that doesn't mean that it should be any the less frequent. As I said before, such prayer is made in the length of the spirit, so it never ceases until it gets what it is longing for. We can see this in the example of the man or woman who is frightened in the way I mentioned earlier. They never stop shouting their little words "help!" or "fire!" until they have found some remedy for their distress.

Chapter 40: Don't Analyze These Words

In the same way, fill your heart with the spiritual meaning of the word "sin" without considering any particular kind of sin, mortal or venial, like pride, anger or envy, covetousness, sloth, gluttony, or lust. What on earth does it matter to contemplatives what kind of sin or how bad it is? While they are engaged in contemplation all sins seem equally grave to them because even the smallest sin separates them from God and deprives them of interior peace.

So you should experience sin as a kind of lump — never mind of what — that is inseparable from *you*. Then keep uttering this one cry in your heart without ceasing: "Sin, sin, sin! Out, out, out!" You can learn this spiritual cry directly from God by experience far better than from other men or by precept. It is most effective when it remains an entirely spiritual utterance and is neither conceptualized nor put into words, except on occasion, when a full heart bursts spontaneously into speech, and body and soul are united in the experience of the sorrowful encumbrance of sin.

Use the little word "God" in [this] way. Fill your heart with the spiritual meaning of the word without thinking about any of his particular works, wondering whether it is good, better, or the best of all his attributes or whether this divine effect is experienced in body or spirit or in a special virtue infused by grace into a man's soul. Don't think about this divine effect as humility, charity, patience or abstinence, hope, faith, sobriety, chastity, or voluntary poverty. What on earth does this matter to contemplatives? They discover and experience all the virtues in God because everything is found in him: he created it and keeps it in existence. Contemplatives believe that if they have God they have all good things and so never covet any particular thing but only the good God himself. You must do the same, as far as grace permits you. Direct your whole heart and soul to God in his fullness, so that your mind and will are both engaged with God alone.

Furthermore, as long as you live this pitiful life you are bound to experience this foul, putrid lump of sin that is in some sense inseparable from yourself, so you can use these two words "sin" and "God" interchangeably. You will have this underlying realization that if you only had God you would have no sin and if you were able to rid yourself of sin, you would have God.

Chapter 43: A Naked Awareness of Self

Make sure that there is nothing stirring in your mind and will but God alone. Try to hack down all knowledge or experience of anything less than God and trample them thoroughly under the cloud of forgetting. You must understand that in contemplation you not only have to forget all other creatures apart from yourself (what they have done — and even what you have done yourself!) but that you must also forget yourself and all the good works that you have done for God's sake. A perfect lover is one who not only loves his beloved more than himself but in some sense hates himself for the sake of the beloved.

This is how you must treat yourself: you must feel that anything that agitates your mind or will except God is hateful and tedious. After all, whatever it is it interposes itself between you and your God, so no wonder you are filled with loathing and contempt for yourself when you inevitably experience sin as a disgusting and putrid lump (never mind what kind of sin it is!) that separates you from God. That lump you experience is simply yourself, and you should think of it as solidly frozen into your inmost being. It is identified with you and will never let you go.

So stamp down all knowledge and experience of anything whatsoever; above all you should concentrate on forgetting yourself. Your understanding and experience of everything else depends on your knowledge of yourself, and it is far easier to forget other creatures once you have laid yourself to one side. If you try really hard to prove this, you will discover that once you have forgotten all other creatures and their deeds— and all your own affairs, too—there remains between you and your God a naked apprehension of your essential being. This must go, too, before you can fully experience true contemplation.

Chapter 44: The Death of the Ego

Now you are going to ask me how you can destroy this stark awareness of yourself. You might be thinking that if you destroy this sense of yourself, you will destroy everything else too, and you will be right. But I will answer this fear by telling you that without a very special grace from God and without a particular aptitude on your part, you will never be able to get rid of this naked sense of self. For your part, this aptitude consists of a robust and profound sorrow of spirit.

But it is essential that you exercise discretion in this matter. You mustn't put any excessive strain on your body or soul but should, as it were, sit quietly, almost as if you were asleep and entirely saturated and immersed in sorrow. This is what true and complete sorrow is like, and if you can achieve it you will find that it helps you. Everybody has a special reason for grief, but the person who has a deep experience of himself existing far apart from God feels the most acute sorrow. Any other grief seems trivial in comparison. Indeed, anybody who has never experienced this grief should be really sorry for himself, because he has never felt perfect

sorrow! Once we have acquired this sorrow it not only purifies our souls, but it takes away all the pain merited by sin and
thus makes the soul capable of receiving that joy that takes
from a man all sense of his own being.

If this sorrow is genuine, it is full of holy longing.
Otherwise nobody could bear it. Unless a soul is nourished
from time to time with some of the consolations of contemplation, he could never endure this knowledge and experience of his nature. Whenever he longs to have a true
experience of God in purity of heart (as far as he can here
below), inevitably he finds that he experiences instead this
foul, putrid lump of self, which he must entirely reject and
forsake if he would be a true disciple, as God himself taught
on the Mount of Perfection. Thus, he is doomed to become
almost mad with grief, so much so that he weeps and wails,
struggles, curses and reviles himself, and, in short, it seems
that the burden of self is so insupportable that he doesn't
care what happens to him as long as God's will be done. And
yet in all this grief, he never wants to stop living, because
that would be an insanity inspired by the devil and a rejection of God himself. Rather, he wants to go on living and he
is fully determined to be grateful to God for the great gift of
his creation, even though he longs ceaselessly to lose all
sense of his own existence.

Everybody should know and experience this sorrowful
weariness with self in some way or other. God promises to
teach his spiritual disciples according to his good pleasure,
but there must be a corresponding readiness in the disciple's
own soul and body as he ascends the ladder of contemplation
and cultivates the right disposition before he can be wholly
united to God in perfect love — or as perfectly as possible in
this world — if God wills.

From Chapter 45: Dangers of the Contemplative Life

But I must warn you about one thing. It is very easy for a young contemplative, who is inexperienced and has not been tested in the spiritual life, to be deceived. Unless he is careful and does not get the grace to take care and humbly seek advice, it is possible that he may suffer physical damage, fall into spiritual delusions, and become proud, sensual, and a seeker of weird and wonderful mortal states.

This is how it happens. A young man or woman, who has recently entered this school of piety, hears about sorrow and longing: how a man must raise his heart to God and yearn incessantly to experience divine love. Immediately their trivial minds understand this in a material and physical sense, instead of spiritually as it was intended. So they put a quite excessive strain on their nervous systems. Because they lack grace and are proud and censorious, they strain in such crude, material ways that in no time at all they become hysterical, exhausted, or fall into an unhealthy lethargy. To find relief of body and soul they try to escape into some useless exterior sensual or material pleasure. If they don't fall into this trap, they experience, quite deservedly because of their spiritual blindness and the irritation of their natural powers (theirs is a purely physical, not a spiritual work), an unnatural glow in their breasts. This has been caused by their abuse of the body in this false type of contemplation. Again, the devil, the enemy of their souls, can inspire a false ardor in their breasts because of their pride, their sensual outlook, and their empty curiosity. Yet they can think it is the fire of love, kindled and nurtured by the grace and kindness of the Holy Ghost! Indeed, many evils are caused by this self-deception: hypocrisy, heresy, and error. Following fast on the heels of such bad experience comes false knowledge in the devil's school, just as true knowledge in God's school succeeds the right kind of experience. I tell you, truthfully, that the devil as well as God has his own contemplatives.

Chapter 46: Don't Put Too Much Strain on Yourself

So for the love of God be careful in this work and do not put too much strain on yourself, emotionally, beyond what you can bear. Eagerness is more effective in this matter than a show of useless force. The more eagerly you work, the more humble and spiritual you become, whereas the more crude force you employ, the more physical and animal. So be careful, for any brutish heart that presumes to touch the high mountain of contemplation will be beaten away with stones. Stones are hard and dry: whatever they hit they hurt. Similarly, crude striving is inseparable from a more physical, material struggle and is dry from the lack of grace. They hurt the unintelligent soul very badly and it can fester in diabolical delusions. So keep this crude force at bay and learn to love eagerly, with a pliable, serious demeanor of body and soul. Wait upon the will of our Lord humbly and courteously and don't grab at experience like a greedy greyhound, however hungry you are. You can make a game of it: do whatever you can to conceal the crude restlessness of your soul as though you were determined not to let him know how much you long to see him, to possess him, to experience him.

You probably think that I am talking childishly and playfully, but I really believe that anyone who has the grace to do as I say and enter into the spirit of it would have a delightful game with God, rather as a father plays with his child, kissing and hugging him and glad to do so.

Chapter 71: Moses and Aaron

Some people think that this kind of contemplation is so difficult and frightening that it cannot be achieved without a great deal of hard work beforehand, that it can only be managed occasionally and in moments of ecstasy. I can only answer such people in an apparently feeble manner, saying that it all depends on the will of God and his good pleasure and whether they have the spiritual ability to receive the gift of contemplation and to undertake this labor of spirit.

There are indeed some people who cannot attain this state without a long and energetic spiritual struggle, and even then they only attain it infrequently, in response to a special vocation from our Lord, which is called "ecstasy." And there are others who are so spiritually talented and at ease with God and at home in contemplation that they can enter this state whenever they like as though it were a normal thing: when they are sitting, walking, standing, or kneeling. Yet at the same time they are in full possession of their faculties of body and soul and can, if they like, even use them with some — though not excessive — difficulty. Moses is an example of the first kind of person, and Aaron, the high priest of the Temple, the other, because in the Old Testament the Ark of the Covenant prefigures the gift of contemplation and contemplatives are prefigured by the people who took care of the Ark, as the story shows. This is a good comparison, because just as all the jewels and relics of the Temple were contained in the Ark, so in this little act of love directed to the cloud of unknowing is contained all the virtues of the human soul, the spiritual temple of God.

Before Moses was able to see the Ark and learn how it should be constructed, he had to make a long and wearisome effort to climb to the peak of the mountain and there for six days he lived and worked in a cloud, waiting until the seventh day when God was ready to reveal to him the way in which the Ark should be made. In Moses' long struggle and delayed revelation we can see those who do not complete this spiritual work without a long preliminary struggle, and even then they achieve it only occasionally, only when God is prepared to grant them this grace.

But what Moses saw only infrequently and with great effort, Aaron was able to see in the divine revelation in the Temple beyond the Veil as often as he chose to enter it, by virtue of his office. In Aaron we see those people I mentioned earlier, who attain perfect contemplation whenever they like, because of their spiritual genius and with the help of God's grace.

Chapter 74: The Author Takes His Leave

Now if you think that this kind of prayer will not suit your physical or spiritual temperament, it will be no discredit to you to abandon it and adopt another method with a good spiritual director. In that case, I beg you to excuse me, because my only intention was to help you in this book with such simple knowledge as I possess. So read it over carefully two or three times; the more you read it, the better you will understand it. You may find that a sentence that you found very difficult on the first or second reading becomes easy the next time.

Yes! I cannot believe that anybody who has adopted the contemplative life will not feel some sympathy for the outcome of this method when they read or speak about it, or hear it read or spoken of. So if it seems to do you good, thank God with all your heart and for the love of God pray for me.

Press on with this work, therefore. And I beg you, for the love of God, not to let anybody see this book unless you think that he is likely to profit from it, as the book describes when it says what kind of people should attempt contemplation and when they should begin. If you let suitable people see it, I beg you to tell them to take their time over it, because perhaps some of the material — in the beginning or the middle — left, as it were, hanging in midair, is not fully explained in the immediate context. But if it is not dealt with immediately, it will be explained soon afterward or at the end. So if somebody sees only one part of the book and not another there is a chance that he could easily fall into error. Therefore, I beg you to work as I direct you. If there is anything here that you would like explained more fully, let me know what it is and I shall do my poor best to put you right.

But I really do not want censorious and contentious people or those addicted to gossip to read this book. I had no intention of writing for them and so I would rather they heard nothing about it — nor those learned (or ignorant!) people who want knowledge for its own sake. Yes, I mean it; even if they are good men, well-employed in the active life, this book is not their business.

Chapter 75: A Final Encouragement

Not all those people who read or hear the contents of this book read aloud or explained and like the sound of it or get a good feeling while they are reading it are called to contemplation. It could be that this feeling is merely inspired by natural curiosity rather than grace.

But if they want to test this feeling to see where it comes from, they can try it in this way, if they like. First, let them see if they have completed all the preliminaries, by purifying their conscience according to the decrees of Holy Church and the advice of their spiritual director. So far, so good. But if they want to examine themselves more closely, let them see if this method of prayer comes to mind more habitually than other spiritual exercises. If they realize that their conscience does not approve of their actions, physical or spiritual, unless this hidden little impulse of love comes to the fore, then it is a sign that God is calling them to this kind of prayer; otherwise he is certainly not doing so.

I am not saying that people who have this vocation never think about anything else. No, indeed! A young apprentice in the spiritual life often finds that his consciousness of this impulse is withdrawn, for several reasons. Sometimes it happens so that he does not depend upon it presumptuously and think that it is in his power to produce it whenever he wants. This is pride. Whenever we lose a consciousness of grace, pride is the reason for it — not necessarily actual pride but the potential pride that could fill the soul if it were not sometimes deprived of the consolations of grace. And that is why some young fools think that God is their enemy, when he is really their best friend.

Sometimes it is withheld because of their carelessness. When that happens they soon experience an intensely bitter pain that wracks them grievously. Sometimes our Lord cleverly makes us wait, so as to increase it by this delay and make us value it more when we have found and experienced it again after its loss. And this is one of the chief and most trustworthy signs a soul can have that he is called to contemplation, if, after such a period when he has not been able to contemplate for a long time, it suddenly comes back without any effort on his part: he finds that he has a greater and more ardent desire and longing for contemplation than ever before. So much so, I have often believed, that he is more glad to have found it again than he was sorry to have lost it.

If this happens it is an infallible sign that God has called him to be a contemplative, whatever kind of person he is or has been in his past life.

For it is not what you are nor what you have been that God regards with his most merciful eyes, but what you would like to be. As St. Gregory says, "all holy desires are only increased by delay: if they decrease because of delay they were never holy desires!" If somebody feels less and less joy in new discoveries and an unexpected resurgence of old desires that he had once carefully cultivated, these desires may have been good but they were not holy. St. Augustine describes holy desire when he says that the whole life of a good Christian consists simply of a holy desire.

Farewell, spiritual friend, and may God's blessing and mine be upon you! I pray almighty God that true peace, wise counsel, and spiritual consolation with abundant grace be with you and with all of us who love God in this life forever, Amen.

III

Walter Hilton

alter Hilton was probably the most influential of our mystics. Manuscripts of his treatise *The Ladder of Perfection* were passed from monastery to monastery and were soon found as far afield as southern France. But even though his book was intended for contemplatives, it was also widely read by laymen and -women. As the most popular spiritual English classic, it helped to form the religious outlook of Catholics in England right up to the Reformation. *The Ladder of Perfection* may lack the charm of some of the other works anthologized here, but it was the first systematic and comprehensive account of the spiritual life to be written in English and its immediate popularity shows that it answered a real need. Many people today also find it the most accessible and the least esoteric of the English mystical works of the fourteenth century.

We know very little about Hilton himself, however. He was probably an Augustinian canon of Thurgarton Priory near Newark in Nottinghamshire and died on March 24, 1396. It was thought for a long time that he was a Carthusian, but there is no firm evidence for this. The Carthusians, a reformed branch of the Benedictine order, were particularly enthusiastic about *The Ladder of Perfection*, and this tells us something important about the nature of Hilton's achievement. The Carthusians lived — and still live — a more solitary contemplative life than their Benedictine brethren, but retain certain traditional and communal monastic observances. Their solitary life meant that they were in the forefront of the new mystical spirit of the fourteenth century, and Hilton helped them to graft the new spirituality onto the old Benedictine pieties. *The Ladder of Perfection* is divided into two parts: the first deals with the preparation that is necessary before the novice is ready for advanced contemplation, and the second deals with the mystical experience. Hilton was certainly conscious of writing for a wide monastic audience, but *The Ladder of Perfection* is ostensibly written for a nun who was enclosed in a convent and bound by traditional monastic disciplines, but who also seemed about to begin a more solitary life. Like the Carthusians she needed help to wed the old and new forms of spirituality so that her new contemplative vocation was not a painful dislocation from the past.

The solitary life did not mean that a contemplative was deprived of all human contact, however. Enclosed monks and nuns, hermits and anchoresses, were sought out by the secular clergy and by the laity for advice and help. They offered in effect a free counseling service, and many of the problems brought to them were of a spiritual nature, which in itself showed the high level of spiritual and religious interest in England during the fourteenth century. It is a reminder that Chaucer and Langland do not give us the total picture. Hilton clearly attached great importance to this apostolate: he tells his nun that she will meet God in her visitors just as surely as in the solitude of her cell. But he also warns her not to let these spiritual conversations degenerate into gossip — an obvious danger and one that could ruin the religious life. In the sixteenth century, St. Teresa of Ávila complained bitterly of the

perils of the parlor in her fashionable convent, where the nuns
practically ran a salon!

The first part of *The Ladder of Perfection* discusses the early
stages of the religious development of a contemplative in a
monastic context. Hilton calls this stage the "reformation of
faith" and declares that it is the bedrock and indispensable
preparation for the mystical life. This spiritual transformation is seen as an active struggle on the part of a religious
(who is, of course, assisted by grace) to rid the soul of sin
and impurity. It is an attempt to conform to a divine reality
and standard that the soul cannot "see" at this early stage but
that she has to take on faith. The ascetic and penitential
purification was also seen by *The Cloud of Unknowing* as an
essential prelude to the contemplative life together with the
related monastic disciplines of *Lectio, Meditatio,* and *Oratio.*
But *The Cloud of Unknowing* does not discuss these in its
monograph. Hilton, however, devotes a considerable part of
the first section of *The Ladder of Perfection* to these practices,
which a modern reader could easily misunderstand.

Since the sixth century, the Benedictine monks of Europe had evolved a uniquely Western spirituality, which cen-
tered around these disciplines. *Lectio,* or Reading, was
considered essential for prayer (*Oratio*); it enabled a monk to
enter into himself and discover what had to be changed in the
light of divine truth. It was not a grim, agonizing program but
was undertaken in a calm and relaxed way. Monks were
supposed to enjoy *Lectio*: in the scriptures and in the writings
of the fathers of the Church, the monk had an encounter with
the divine and felt that he was in some mysterious sense
studying God himself. Muslims evolved a very similar attitude
toward the Qur'an. As the monk studied God's Word he
would frequently find his heart lifting itself up to God for a
few brief but intense moments. This prayer (*Oratio*) was the
goal of *Lectio* but it was not a prolonged exercise. The Bene-

dictines believed that prayer should be *brevis, pura,* and *frequens* — brief, pure, and frequent. The intensity of these aspirations meant that they were inevitably "brief" and "pure," and the constant reading ensured that they would be "frequent." In *Lectio,* therefore, God revealed himself, and in *Oratio* the monk offered himself to God.

Hilton is writing for a nun for whom *Lectio* is apparently impossible, even though she was obviously able to read. Convents of mere women probably did not have much access to precious books in those days before printing. But we can see the influence of this traditional Western monastic spirituality in Hilton's discussion of verbal prayer. His nun is bound by her order to recite the Divine Office, which St. Benedict had called the *opus dei,* the work of God, at eight appointed "hours" that regularly punctuated her day. Each "hour" — Matins, Lauds, Vespers, and so on — consisted of psalms, prayers, and readings from Scripture and the fathers, and so it gave the nun a form of *Lectio.* Hilton warns her not to skimp these obligatory verbal prayers in her enthusiasm for the new contemplation. They are shaping her mind with God's sacred Word. From time to time, he says, she will be moved to speak to God directly in the brief, intense ejaculations of *Oratio.*

The modern reader is likely to be particularly confused by Hilton's discussion of *Meditatio,* the third great monastic practice. Today we use the word "meditation" quite differently: in Hilton's time it meant study rather than a purely contemplative exercise. It was more like Jewish rabbinical study, where students chant the words of the Talmud aloud as they memorize them, rather than the silent, interior disciplines of a Buddhist monk. In *Meditatio* the Christian monk committed the divine words of his *Lectio* to memory as he pondered their meaning and, as he did so, he recited them aloud. This was not a dreary exercise: rabbinical students feel that chanting the sacred words reveals the inner music to the soul, and learning something "by heart"—a revealing phrase—helps one to interiorize it and make it one's own. In the Middle Ages, people often depicted their monks as ruminative animals, chewing over the Word of God repeatedly, as it were, rolling the words around in their mouths and absorbing it into themselves just as they received Jesus the Word in the Eucharist, in a symbolic and sacramental manner. The result of this *Meditatio* was that the monk or nun experienced the truths of faith in an entirely new way. It was a process of rediscovery and re-vision in which the deeper significance of familiar truths flashed into new life. When Hilton talks about *Meditatio*, therefore, he is not using the word as a Christian would use it today. He is describing the sudden new apprehension of divine truth bestowed upon people who have just embarked on the spiritual life when they are rediscovering the truths of their faith during their periods of study. They will, he suggests, gain a new appreciation of the meaning of sin or a fresh sympathy with the Passion of Christ.

In the early Middle Ages, *Lectio*, *Meditatio*, and *Oratio* were all designed to lead to Contemplation, but *Contemplatio* was not regarded as an esoteric discipline, an advanced state of prayer, or the cultivation of an alternative mode of consciousness. *Contemplatio* was traditionally an attitude of constant attention to God. It was certainly not a highly emotional state, nor was it an abandonment of old modes of perception. The regular, monotonous monastic disciplines gave the monks a peace and equanimity, which they saw as a tranquil experience of God that was fully in tune with their normal lives. But by the fourteenth century, contemplation had become something very different, and in the second part of his book, Hilton explained to his nun what the modern, innovative Contemplation involved.

This more advanced type of prayer, which, in Hilton's view, was only for monks and nuns, is called "the reformation of feeling." Since Hilton is at pains to show that true contemplation had nothing to do with the emotions and clearly disapproves of Rolle's spirituality, the term seems puzzling. But the "reformation of feeling" is a literal translation of St. Paul's words, *Reformamini in novitate sensus vestri*,[1] as they appeared in the Vulgate — St. Jerome's Latin translation of the Bible. The word *sensus* can be translated as "feeling or experience." The Jerusalem Bible translates this verse: "let your behavior change, modeled by your new mind." Hilton interprets "new mind" or "new feeling" as the creation of contemplation, which now demanded far more than the old Benedictine ideal, where the monk did not experience God in the achievement of higher states of consciousness but in the mundane details of daily life.

Like Dame Julian, Hilton was inspired by the theology of the scholastic theologians of the thirteenth century. It quite frequently happens that mystics are deeply influenced by philosophy, even though they tend to decry "the meddling intellect." Kabbalists and Sufis were often moved by the ideas of the Jewish and Muslim rationalists, which they translated into a mystical mode. In much the same way, Hilton and Dame Julian were both inspired by the scholastic rediscovery of St. Augustine's theology of the Trinity, which, St. Thomas Aquinas said, was "the fruit and goal of our entire life."[2] They did not engage in an abstruse discussion of the technicalities of Trinitarianism but saw it as a paradigm of the religious experience of God. The Kabbalists developed a similar mythical conception of the inner life of God in their depiction of the world of the *Sephirot,* the divine spheres that emanated from the unknowable God and enabled him to be known by man: these emanations provided man with the means of ascending to the deity. In St. Augustine's interpretation of Trinitarian doctrine, Hilton also found a way of showing how sinful man could learn about the incomprehensible God and return to his creator. It explained the shape of the mystical experience that came to him in prayer. Mystical experience never arrives out of the blue; it is always influenced by the religious milieu of the mystic, even though he may want to transcend the beliefs and attitudes that he found there.

St. Augustine taught that God had created man in his own image and so it was by looking at his own soul that man would discover God: "May I know myself! May I know thee!"[3] he had cried. There was a trinity within each one of us consisting of the three powers of the soul that corresponded to the three divine Persons: memory, understanding, and will; it enabled us to be, to know, and to love what we are in the same way as God knows and loves himself. By learning to know his soul, therefore, man would achieve a vision of God himself, albeit in a glass darkly. Hilton now urged his contemplatives to look into their own depths and, by means of the disciplines of contemplation — the "reformation of feeling" — to refashion the image of God there that had been destroyed by original sin.

But the inner reformation demanded that we abandon our old earthbound modes of perception and to depict this process Hilton uses the metaphor of the pilgrimage. In itself, this showed the direction in which European spirituality was heading. Earlier the physical journey of the pilgrimage had been one of the chief disciplines by means of which the Cluniacs had managed to reshape the consciousness of Europe. By the fourteenth century the pilgrimage to Jerusalem, City of Peace, had become an interior journey to the depths of the self. During the journey away from his old un-reformed self, the mystic has to enter a dark night of the senses. Hilton tells him to wait patiently in the darkness and acclimatize himself to this new existence, stripped of all the things that had made life worthwhile before. Hilton's dark night is clearly similar to "the cloud of unknowing," and it seems that he was familiar with the older work. But his description of the journey to Jerusalem is even closer to the Ascent of Mount Carmel, described in the sixteenth century by St. John of the Cross. John also tells the mystic that, if he wants to approach God, he must cast aside every single scrap of knowledge he owns and divest himself of all his own ideas and opinions:

> *The soul must journey by knowing God through what he is not, rather than through what he is, it must journey, insofar as possible, by way of the denial and rejection of natural and supernatural apprehensions. This is our task now with the memory. We must draw it away from its natural props and capacities and raise it above itself (above all distinct knowledge and apprehensible possession) to supreme hope in the incomprehensible God.[4]*

John describes the agony of the ensuing dark night of the soul, but Hilton writes more calmly and with an acceptance of this dereliction that is required by all mystical traditions. All over the world, mystics had told the adept that he must die to himself and to all that he knows; he must experience annihilation and extinction, which the Sufis call *'fana*. Only then will he rise again to an entirely different life in the Reality that exists beyond thought.

The modern reader may feel that, like our other mystics, Walter Hilton dwells too much on sin for twentieth-century taste. We are understandably wary of any religiosity that encourages too much guilt and anxiety. Indeed, Christians in Europe tended to concentrate far too much on their own failings — a tendency that would later drive Luther to the brink of despair. St. Augustine, who can be regarded as the founder of Western Christianity, created the doctrine of Original Sin in the fifth century: The first sin of Adam and Eve had been transmitted to all their descendents so that humanity was chronically flawed and each one of us was doomed to eternal damnation unless we were baptized into the saving death of Jesus Christ. There is nothing like this pessimistic doctrine in either Judaism or Islam, and Greek Orthodox Christians never wholly accepted it, but it had a profound influence on the Western spirit — not least in the Puritanism that was so influential in America. This was a weakness in Western Christianity and many people in the West are right to lay this burden aside. Too great a sense of sin can paralyze us and embed us in the egotism we seek to transcend. Yet none of our mystics dwell on sin nearly as much as their contemporaries. Walter Hilton was deeply affected by Augustine's theology and he would have accepted the doctrine of Original Sin as a matter of course. He concentrates far more, however, on God and on practical ways of overcoming the inherent selfishness and apathy that most of us experience in ourselves and that impedes our spiritual progress. Like the author of *The Cloud of Unknowing,* Hilton does not want his reader to agonize about her failings but to work calmly to leave them behind and progress to her final goal.

Like the other English mystics, Hilton does not want the contemplative to agonize and strain unduly. He makes the point that the love of God is not an emotion that we have to drum up in ourselves. It is the Holy Spirit at work in our souls, a gift of the divine Love of the Trinity, which enables us to love God with the same love whereby he loves himself. Again, this is a common mystical theme. It is memorably expressed in an Islamic mode in the famous sacred tradition (*hadith qudsi*), which makes God say that when one of his human servants turns to him:

I love him and when I love him, I am the Hearing wherewith he heareth, and the Sight wherewith he seeth and the Hand whereby he graspeth and the Foot whereon he walketh.

The calm approach of Hilton and his contemporaries to the mystical extremity may not have been simply due to British phlegm but may also have been the legacy of the relaxed and tranquil spirituality of Benedictine monasticism. It was Hilton's impressive achievement to root the new mysticism firmly in the old.

The Ladder of Perfection

Book 1. Chapter 1: My Sister in Jesus Christ

I beg you, my spiritual sister in Jesus Christ, to be satisfied with your vocation and devote yourself faithfully to the service to which our Lord has called you. Strive energetically and make every possible effort to make the outward state of religion, which you show to the world, a reality in the integrity of your good life. Since you have forsaken the world and are like a corpse in the eyes of other people, your whole physical, external life turned now toward our Lord, make sure, so to speak, that your heart is also dead to earthly fears and desires and turned wholly toward our lord Jesus Christ. You are well aware that turning to God externally without a correspondent movement of the heart is just a picture or simulacrum of virtue — there is no truth in it. Wretched indeed is that man or woman who abandons all interior discipline and conforms only externally, making an empty show of holiness in behavior, speech, and outward actions, looking always at what other people are doing and judging their faults, thinking themselves to be something whereas in fact they are nothing and have simply taken themselves in. Don't you become like this but turn body and soul to God and conform interiorly to his likeness by means of humility, charity, and the other spiritual virtues. Then you really will have turned to him.

I don't say that you will be able to turn to him spiritually on the very first day of your religious life with a full array of virtues as easily as you have been physically enclosed in your convent. But I want you to understand that the reason why you have been enclosed physically in this way is that you may enter a more perfect spiritual cloister. Just as your body has now been shut away from the physical society of men, so too your heart should be cloistered from carnal fears and any desire for the things of this world. It is to help you to reach this state that I am going to set down my ideas in this little book.

Chapter 12: Feelings and Exotic Emotions Are Worthless in Contemplation

What binds and unites Jesus to a soul is a good will and a great desire for him alone, a desire to possess him and see him spiritually in his full beatitude. The greater this desire, the more strongly is Jesus fastened to the soul; the less the desire, the more loosely is he bound. So any inspiration or emotion that diminishes this longing and seeks to drag it down from a constant recollection of Jesus Christ and from the ascent to him that our true nature demands, will cut Jesus off and break his connection with the soul. It does not come from God, therefore, but from the enemy. But on the other hand if any inspiration, emotion, or revelation increases this desire and ties the knot of love and devotion to Jesus more tightly, opens the eyes of the soul to a clearer spiritual knowledge and makes it assess its powers more humbly, this inspiration comes from God. You already have some idea of how important it is not to allow your heart to rest consciously or take a consuming delight in those kinds of consolations and pleasant experiences that are felt by the senses, no matter how good they seem. You must reckon that they are of little or no account compared with the spiritual desire and constant recollection of Jesus Christ. Don't set your heart on them too much, but, if you can, forget all about them.

Instead, try to arrive in your prayers at a more spiritual experience of God: that is, to know the wisdom of God, the boundless power of Jesus Christ and his great goodness in himself and in his creatures. This is true contemplation and the other kinds of emotional experience are worthless. As St. Paul says, *In caritate radicati, et fundati, ut possitis comprehendere cum omnibus sanctis quae sit logitudo, et latitudo, sublimitas, et profundum*,[5] that is, "Be rooted and founded in love, not that you may know a physical sound or sweet taste in your mouth or anything physical like that but that you may know and experience like all truly holy people the length of God's endless being, the breadth of his astonishing love and goodness, the height of his sublimity, and the bottomless depth of his wisdom."

Chapter 15: Preparation for Contemplation

There are three established ways of achieving contemplation: the study of scripture and doctrine, spiritual meditation, and constant and devout prayer [Lectio, Meditatio, and Oratio]. You are not really able to read the scriptures for yourself, so you must rely on prayer and meditation. By meditation you will come to appreciate how weak you are in virtue, and prayer will help you to acquire it. In meditation you will see what a poor creature you are and discover your sins and failings — pride, covetousness, gluttony, and lust, the wicked emotions of envy, anger, hatred, gloom, irritability, bitterness, laziness, and irrational depression. You will also realize that your heart is full of false regrets and fears that spring from a worldly, carnal outlook. All these emotions will well up from your heart as water flows constantly from the spring of a polluted well and they will block your spiritual vision so that you can neither see nor experience the pure love of Jesus Christ.

You must understand that until your heart is thoroughly purified of such sins by a firm grasp of truth and by a constant interior vision of the earthly life of Christ, you cannot have a truly spiritual experience of God. Look what he says in the Gospel, *Beati mundo corde quoniam ipsi Deum videbunt*[6]: "Blessed are the pure of heart for they shall see God." You will also see the virtues that you must acquire in the course of your meditation — humility, tranquillity, patience, rectitude, fortitude, temperance, purity, peace and sobriety, faith, love, and charity. In meditation you will see how good, beautiful, and beneficial such virtues are and by means of prayer you will long for them and acquire them, for without them you will never become a contemplative. As Job says, *In abundantia ingredieris sepulcrum,*[7] that is to say, "you must enter your grave [that is, contemplation] by means of an abundance of good deeds and spiritual virtues."

Chapter 26: Don't Listen to People Who Talk About "The Fire of Love"

None of the people who talk about "the fire of love" really know what it is, and I certainly can't explain it, but I can tell you this: it is not a physical heat that can be experienced by our senses. It is true that a soul can experience it while it is still in the body during prayer and spiritual exercises, but not in a physical way. It may be that when this fire is at work in the soul the body may experience some heat, which seems to be sparked off by the correspondent spiritual activity, but the fire of love itself is *not* a physical thing but simply the spiritual longing of the soul. Men and women who have experienced true devotion have no doubt about this, but some of them are a bit simpleminded and imagine that because it is called a fire it must be as hot as a physical fire.

Chapter 27: Vocal Prayer

Now about your question about the kind of prayer that is best for you: I will give you my opinion.

You must understand that there are three kinds of prayer: the first consists of words that God has composed himself, like the Lord's Prayer and those that have been prescribed for everybody by Holy Church: Matins, Evensong, and the other "hours" of the office. There are also those prayers that have been composed by holy men addressed to our Lord, our Lady, and the saints. I think that this kind of prayer, which is known as "Vocal Prayer," is extremely useful for a person like yourself, a religious bound by the rule and custom of your Order to recite Matins and the Divine Office as devoutly as you can. For whenever you chant Matins, you begin with the Lord's Prayer and then to inspire you to greater devotion, it has also been decreed that you recite the psalms, hymns, and other prayers that have, like the Lord's Prayer, been inspired by the Holy Spirit. So don't rush through these vocal prayers carelessly, as though it was a dreary duty, but gather all your thoughts and feelings together to help you to recite these prayers with greater seriousness and devotion than any of your own private prayers. You should be aware that because this is the prayer of Holy

Church no other prayer is more useful to you than this type of Vocal Prayer. So you must not allow yourself to be bored and then, with the help of grace, you will transform an obligation into a voluntary act and so, again by means of grace, this obligation will liberate you instead of inhibiting your spiritual aspirations. After you have recited these prescribed prayers, you can add others like the Lord's Prayer if you wish. I think that the prayers that you personally like best and that you find bring you the most spiritual consolation are the best ones to use.

This kind of prayer is especially helpful to somebody who has just embarked on the spiritual life, and it is better than any other kind of spiritual exercise. For at the beginning a man is unsubtle, crude, and sense-bound in his approach, unless he is given a special grace, and he cannot engage in truly spiritual thoughts in meditation because his soul has not yet been purified from his old sins. That is why I think it is more profitable for somebody at this stage to recite the Lord's Prayer, the Hail Mary, and read the psalms and other similar prayers. For someone who cannot run easily in the paths of spiritual prayer because his feet of knowledge and love that have to carry him have been infected by sin needs a trusty staff to support him. This staff is the special prayer ordained by God and Holy Church to help men's souls. With this kind of prayer, the soul of a worldly man, who is always sliding into earthbound thoughts and emotions perceived by the body, can be elevated and raised above himself. He will depend upon it like a staff and it will discipline and nourish him with the sweet words of the prayer as a child is nourished with milk. In this way he will not lapse into error or fantasy in his empty meditations. There is nothing in this kind of prayer to deceive somebody who has made up his mind to labor in it continuously and humbly.

Chapter 28: It Is Dangerous to Abandon the Discipline of Vocal Prayer Too Early

It follows that people — if there be people like this — who give up Vocal Prayer and other disciplines of the body too early and concentrate on meditation at the very beginning of their religious lives or the second they have received a little spiritual consolation of feeling and knowledge are most unwise: they have not been properly established in the spiritual life. In other parts of their meditation they often imagine that they have had a spiritual experience or they manufacture "spiritual" thoughts for themselves that correspond to their own sense-bound experiences, which have not been inspired by grace. And so, because they are lacking in discretion, they put too much strain on their minds and weaken their physical health and then fall into fantasy or peculiar delusions or even into downright error. Thus, they obstruct the grace that God wants to give them by indulging these empty devotions. The reason for this is an inner pride and presumption, because once they have experienced a little grace, they imagine that this is of such overwhelming magnitude that they lose their way, falling prey to a dangerous self-aggrandizement. If only they realized how paltry the grace that they have experienced is compared with the grace that God really gives and wants to give us, they would be ashamed to mention it unless they were forced to do so. David speaks of Vocal Prayer in the psalms when he says, *Voce mea ad Dominum clamavi; voce mea deprecatus sum.*[8] To inspire other men to pray with their mouths as well as with their hearts, the Prophet David said: "I cried to God with my voice and with my speech I besought the Lord."

Chapter 29: The Second Kind of Vocal Prayer

The next kind of prayer also uses words but does not consist of any definite or particular utterances. This happens when a man or woman experiences the grace of fervor as a special gift from God and during this experience speaks to him as though he were actually present, using those words that come into his mind to express the feelings in his heart after he has counted his sins and realized his wretchedness, perceived the malice and wiles of the enemy or the goodness and mercy of God. And then he cries to our Lord with longing in his heart and with words in his mouth for help and aid, like a man who is in danger in the midst of enemies or one who is ill and shows his sores to God as though to a doctor, saying like David, *Eripe me de inimicis meis, Deus meus*[9]: "Ah, Lord, deliver me from my enemies!" or *Sana animam mean quia peccavi tibi*[10]: "Ah, Lord, heal my soul for I have sinned against you"—or other words like that which spring to mind. He also sees the goodness, favor, and mercy of God as so immense that he wants to love him with all the affection that his heart can muster and thank him with words and psalms that express his love and praise of God. As David said, *Confitemini Domino quoniam bonus, quoniam in saeculum misericordia eius*[11]: "Love and praise the Lord because he is good and merciful." Or he can use other similar words, depending on what he is moved to say.

Chapter 30: The Experience of Fervor

This kind of prayer pleases God very much because it springs simply from a heartfelt emotion and so it never leaves your lips without success and without resulting in some kind of favor. As I have said earlier, this type of prayer belongs to the second stage of contemplation. Someone who has experienced this gift of fervor from God needs to shun the presence and company of all men for the time being and remain alone, so that he is not prevented from praying. Anyone who has it should hold on to it as long as he can, for it cannot last long. For however pleasant it is, if grace comes to you in abundance it is extraordinarily exhausting spiritually and it is also very wearing to the physical nature of the people who experience it frequently. For if grace comes so powerfully it makes the body thrash around this way and that, like a man who is drunk and cannot find comfort in any position. The intensity of such passionate love shatters all our lust and pleasure in worldly things with violence and force and it wounds the soul with a joyful sword of love. The body collapses under this great onslaught and cannot bear it. This divine touch is so powerful that the most evil, sensual man in the world would sober up if he were really touched just once by this sharp sword and he would seriously apply himself to the spiritual life for a long time afterward. He would hate all the lusts and pleasures of the flesh and all the worldly things that he took such delight in before.

Chapter 32: The Third Kind of Prayer: the Prayer of the Heart

The third kind of prayer arises only in the heart. It comes softly, using no words, together with great peace and quiet of body and soul. Anybody who has ambitions to pray like this must have a pure heart, because it comes to those men and women who have achieved peace of soul either after a long struggle of soul and body or by the sharp blows of love that I have just mentioned. Their passions have been transformed into a taste for spiritual things that enables them to pray without ceasing in their hearts and to love and praise God without being held back by temptations and trifles of the kind I mentioned when I was describing the second stage of contemplation. St. Paul speaks of this kind of prayer when he says, *Nam si orem lingua, spiritus meus orat, mens autem mea sine fructu est. Quid ergo? Orabo et spiritu, orabo et mente; psallam spiritu, psallam et mente*,[12] which can be roughly translated: "If I pray with my tongue alone with determination and spiritual labor, the prayer is profitable but my soul is not nourished because it does not experience the fruit of spiritual sweetness that belongs to real insight. So what must I do?" asks St. Paul, and he answers himself: "I shall pray with effort and a spiritual longing and I shall also pray effortlessly in the deeper reaches of my soul, spiritually tasting the sweetness of love and the vision of God; by means of this experience and vision of God, my soul will be nourished." This is how St. Paul was able to pray, as I understand it. Our Lord speaks symbolically of this type of prayer in Holy Scripture: *Ignis in altare meo semper ardebit, et cotidie sacerdos surgens mane subjicietus ligna, ut lignis non extinguatur.*[13] This can be roughly translated: "The fire of love must always be alight in the soul of a devout and pure man and woman; this is our Lord's altar, and the priest must feed the fire with sticks every morning." This can be interpreted thus: This man must nourish the fire of love in his heart by means of holy psalms, pure thoughts, and an ardent desire so that it never goes out. Our Lord gives this peace to some of his servants. It is as if he wanted to reward their efforts and give them a shadowy glimpse of the love they will enjoy in the bliss of heaven.

Chapter 33: Some Advice for a Beginner

But now you will tell me that I am speaking over your
head when I describe this type of prayer and that it is easy for
me to talk about it but very difficult to do it! You will say that
you cannot pray as devoutly or as wholeheartedly as this,
because whenever you want to lift your mind and heart to
God in prayer so many useless thoughts crowd upon you —
thoughts about things you have done in the past, things you
are going to do, things other people have done, and so on and
so forth. These hold you back and are such a hindrance that
you cannot taste this peace in your prayer nor feel any devotion in the words that you recite. Often the harder you try to
control your heart the less you are able to do so and the more
difficult your prayer is from start to finish. You think, therefore, that it has all been wasted.

To this objection of yours I will reply that I agree that I
talked about this prayer in a way that was too advanced to
you; furthermore, I admit that I have described an experience
that exceeds my own. I mention it, however, for this reason:
you ought to know how we should pray if we did it properly.
And when we cannot manage it like this, we should appreciate
our weakness and beg God for mercy. Our Lord himself
urged this when he said, *Diliges Dominum Deum tuum ex toto
corde tuo, ex tota anima tua, et ex omnibus viribus tuis*[14]: "You shall
love God with all your heart and all your soul and with all
your strength." It is impossible for anybody to fulfill this
commandment as perfectly as it prescribes while living in
this world, and yet our Lord still commanded us to love in this
way. St. Bernard says that he did so for this reason: that we
should thereby recognize our weakness and then humbly cry
for mercy: if we do so we are bound to receive it. But I will
also answer your question with an opinion of my own.

When you come to pray, direct your intention and your

will to God as wholeheartedly and single-mindedly as you can in a brief mental act. Then get to work and do it as well as you can. Even if a myriad of distracting thoughts prevents you from carrying out your original intention, don't be afraid and don't be too angry with yourself or impatient with God, because he has not given you the consolation and spiritual sweetness in your prayer that you imagine he gives to other people. Instead, see this as an example of your weakness and endure it willingly. Keep your prayer, however pathetic it is, firmly in your mind's eye with a humble heart and put your trust in the mercy of our Lord, who is bound to turn this to your good in ways that you cannot conceive. You have to understand that you have discharged your duty and that you will benefit as much from this prayer as from any act of charity that you perform, even if your heart is not in it. So, do what you have to do and let our Lord give you what he wants and don't give him orders. Even if you think that you are careless and negligent and to blame for all this, you must still raise your heart up to God. Because of your failure and for all your other venial sins which cannot be avoided during this wretched life of ours, acknowledge your weakness and beg for mercy, trusting that God will certainly forgive you. Don't struggle any more and don't hang on to your devotions, as though you refused to experience this weakness, with an act of self-control. Leave it and go and do some other good deed, physical or spiritual, and tell yourself that you will do better another time. Even if you fail again in the same old way, a hundred, a thousand times over, do as I tell you and all will be well. Many a soul never experiences any peace of heart in her prayer but struggles all her life against distracting thoughts and is hindered and distressed by them, but if she acts humbly and charitably in other ways she will enjoy a great reward in heaven for her noble efforts.

Chapter 34: Meditation or Study

I must now tell you a little about the way I see meditation. You must understand that there is no definite rule that a
man must constantly obey in his meditations, for these are
gifts of God freely bestowed by him to suit the temperament
of the souls he has chosen and their current state of mind.
Also, when they have made some progress in virtue and in the
religious life, he increases their meditation in both spiritual
knowledge and the love of God to match their progress.
Anybody who is constantly learning about God and the spiritual life seems to grow gradually in the love of God, as we see
in the case of the apostles. On the day of Pentecost when they
were filled with the burning love of the Holy Ghost, they were
not transformed into fools and dolts but became astonishingly
wise in the knowledge of God and skilled in talking about
him: they had reached as high a state as it is possible for
anybody still living in the body. That is what Holy Scripture
says about them: *Repleti sunt omnes Spiritu sancto et coeperunt
loqui magnalia Dei*[15]: "They were all filled with the Holy Spirit
and began to speak of the marvelous deeds of God." All that
knowledge came from their rapturous love of the Holy Spirit
and many meditations.

Our Lord puts many meditations into a man's heart. I
will tell you about some of them, as they appear to me, so that
if you experience any of them you will be better able to work
with them. When somebody whose life had been badly damaged by worldliness and the sins of the flesh begins a new life,
his mind usually dwells most frequently on his sins. With
great contrition and a sorrowful heart, with much weeping
and many tears, he humbly and assiduously begs God for
mercy and forgiveness. If he is so contrite that God can purify
him quite quickly, it seems to him that his sins are always
before his eyes and are so disgusting and horrible that he

cannot bear himself. However good a confession he makes, he still feels his conscience gnawing and plaguing him so that he thinks he has not been fully absolved. He can find no rest and is in such a state of extremity that he would not survive if God in his mercy did not comfort him, as he sees fit, sending him a devotion to his passion or something similar. Our Lord works like this upon the hearts of some people, pretty much as he wills. It shows the great mercy of our Lord, who not only forgives sin but will also forgive his faults and, in return for a short period of suffering the pain of a guilty conscience, he will remit the pains of purgatory. It is also true that if God wants to prepare a man to receive one of his special gifts of love, he must first be scoured and cleansed by the fire of contrition of all the sins of his past life. David speaks of this kind of struggle in many places in the Psalter, especially in the psalm: *Miserere mei Deus, secundum magnam misericordiam tuam*[16]: "Have mercy on me, O God, according to thy great mercy."

Chapter 35: Meditations or Insights About the Life of Christ

Shortly after this struggle, this man — or, indeed, another who has been given the grace to preserve his innocence — receives from our Lord a meditation about his life on earth: either his birth or his passion or a feeling of sympathy with our Lady, St. Mary. When this meditation has been inspired by the Holy Ghost, it is extremely efficacious and will bring you much grace. This sign will tell you if it is genuine: when you are really given a meditation in God, your mind withdraws from all worldly or sensual things and it seems as though you have seen the physical image of the Lord Jesus in your soul as he appeared on earth: how he was captured by

the Jews, bound as a thief, beaten and despised, scourged,
and sentenced to death. You will observe how humbly he
carried the Cross on his back and how cruelly he was nailed to
it; you will also see the crown of thorns on his head and the
sharp spear that pierced his heart. At this spiritual vision, you
will feel your heart moved to such compassion and pity for the
Lord Jesus that you lament and weep, crying with all the
powers of your body and soul, marveling at the goodness and
love, the patience and humility of thy Lord Jesus who was
willing to endure such great pain for a miscreant like you. And
yet for all that, you experience the goodness and mercy of our
Lord so strongly that your heart flies up to him with love and
joy, with many sweet tears and with complete trust that your
sins will be forgiven and your soul saved by virtue of this
precious passion. Whenever such a spiritual vision brings into
your heart the memory of Christ's passion or any other event
of his life with a corresponding emotion in your own breast,
you should know that this is not your doing nor is it the
delusion of one of the evil spirits, but it is caused by the grace
of the Holy Spirit. Like St. Bernard, you can call it a physical
love of God, inasmuch as it is rooted in the physical nature of
Christ. It is extremely good for you and a great way of
acquiring virtue, but it is also a prelude to the contemplation
of the divinity. For nobody can arrive at a spiritual joy in the
contemplation of Christ's divine nature unless he has first
entered imaginatively into the bitterness of his humanity with
compassion and sustained thought. This is what St. Paul did.
First he said, *Nihil judicavi me scire inter vos, nisi Jesum Christum
et hunc crucifixum*[17]: "I spoke to you only of Jesus Christ and
him crucified." That was why he could also say, *Mihi autem
absit gloriari, nisi in cruce Domini nostri Jesu Christi*[18]: "All joy
and pleasure is forbidden me except in the passion of our Lord
Jesus Christ." And after that he could say, *Praedicamus vobis*

Christum Dei virtutem, et Dei sapientiam.[19] All this can be interpreted: "First I preached the humanity and passion of Christ;
now I preach the divinity of Christ to you, the power and
endless wisdom of God."

Chapter 42: Know Thyself!

There is a very helpful and profitable exercise. A man
must enter into himself and get to know his own soul — its
abilities, beauties, and failings. During this interior examination you will come to see the honor and dignity it was meant to
have when it was created and also realize the wretchedness
and evil mess you have fallen into because of your sin. This
vision of self will result in an immense desire and longing
springing up in your heart to recover the dignity and honor
you have lost. You will also feel a loathing and disgust with
yourself and a strong determination to break and suppress
yourself and all the things that hold you back from that
dignity and joy. Anybody who wants to make progress in this
will find it painful and difficult at first, because it is a spiritual
exercise directed against the foundation of all sin, the soil in
which all sins grow, whether they are big or small. This soil is
nothing but an inappropriate and uncontrolled self-love. As
St. Augustine says, all kinds of sin spring from this love,
mortal and venial, and, indeed, unless this soil is dug over and,
as it were, almost dried out by throwing away all carnal and
worldly desires, a soul will never experience the burning love
of Jesus Christ nor attain a clear vision of spiritual matters in
the light of true understanding. A man must undertake this
task to draw his mind away from the fleshly thoughts and
sensual fantasies and also from the love and consciousness of
himself so that the soul can find no rest in any sense-bound

thought or worldly love. For as long as a soul can find no spiritual peace in the love and intimate presence of God it is bound to be in pain. This exercise is difficult and rigorous, but I believe that it is the path commended to those who wanted to become perfect disciples, when he said in the gospel, *Condite intrare per angustam portam; quam arcta est via quae ducit ad vitam, et pauci inveniunt eam*[20]: "Try, therefore, to enter through the narrow gate, for the road that leads to heaven is narrow and only a few find it." Just how exacting this road is our Lord tells us in another place: *Si quis vult venire post me, abneget seipsum et tollat crucem suam et sequatur me. Item qui odit animam suam in hoc mundo, in vitam aeternam costodit eam.*[21] That can be interpreted like this: Whoever wants to come my way must forsake himself and hate even his own soul, which means that he must forsake all love of the flesh and hate his own physical life and its trivial pleasure in the senses for the sake of my love and take up his Cross. That is, endure the pain of this world for a time. Then truly he follows me. This is a hard and narrow road and nothing physical can pass through it, for it demands the death of all sin, as St. Paul says, *Mortificate membra vestra, quae sunt super terram immunditiam, libidinem, concupiscentiam malam*[22]: "Put all your limbs to death in this world, not the limbs of your body but those of the soul, like impurity, lust and an unreasonable attachment to yourself and the things of this world." Thus, all your work hitherto has been to guard against the sins of the flesh and the obvious temptations of the Fiend, coming, so to speak, from outside yourself. Now you must carry this spiritual effort within, to destroy and break the roots of sin in yourself as far as you can. To help you to achieve this more easily, I am going to give you some advice according to my own opinion.

Chapter 43: The Human Soul Is Made in the Likeness of the Trinity

The human soul is a being with three powers: memory, reason or understanding, and will. It was made in the image and likeness of the Trinity, whole, perfect, and sinless. Insofar as our memory was created powerful and strong by virtue of God the Father almighty to enable us to keep him in mind without forgetting him, memory is in the likeness of the Father. Reason was created clear and shining, without error or confusion, as perfect as it is possible in a soul still living in an unglorified body to possess. And so our reason has been made in the image of the Son, who is eternal Wisdom. And our love and will was created pure and ardent for God, without any animal passions of the flesh for any created object, by the sovereign goodness of the Holy Spirit, and, therefore, our will has been made in the likeness of the Holy Spirit, which is holy love. Thus the human soul, which can be called a created trinity, was made perfect in memory, vision, and love by the uncreated blessed Trinity, our Lord. This was the original nature of the human soul, this the dignity, status and honor which God intended for it. This was the status you had in Adam, before man committed his first sin. But when Adam sinned, choosing to love and take pleasure in himself, he lost this honor and dignity in its entirety, as you did in him, and he fell from the holy trinity into a foul, disgusting, wretched trinity — a state of forgetfulness of God, ignorance of him, and an animal lust for himself. It was right that this should happen, for, as David explains it in the Psalter, *Homo, cum in honore esset, non intellexit, comparatus est jumentis insipientibus, et similis factus est illis*[23]: "When a man was still in a state of honor, he did not realize it and so, when he lost it, he became like an animal."

Now, therefore, look and see the pitiable state of your soul. Once your soul was safe in God, but now it has forgotten

him and seeks rest by running from one created thing to
another. He will never be able to find true peace because he
has lost him who is true peace. It is the same with our reason
and with the love which was pure in its pleasure of spiritual
sweetness but which has now become a foul and bestial lust
with a taste for self, created things and the passions of the
flesh; it glories in the senses, as in the sins of gluttony and lust,
and in the imagination — in the sins of pride, vanity, and
covetousness. This fall has been so serious that you can
scarcely perform a single good deed without finding yourself
besmirched with vanity. Nor can you easily use any of your
five senses purely but your heart is seized with a sterile lust
and passion which drives the love of God from your heart. It
can, therefore, never enter into your experience — you have
no spiritual faculty to receive it. Everybody engaged in the
spiritual life knows this all too well.

   This, then, is the sad state of our soul and the evil plight
that has befallen us through the Original Sin of mankind —
leaving aside all the other miseries and sins that you have
voluntarily added yourself. And you must realize that even if
you had personally never committed a single sin — venial or
mortal — during your life on earth but only had this sin, which
is called "original" because it was the first sin committed and
represents the loss of the righteousness you had when you
were originally created, you could never have been saved
unless our Lord Jesus Christ had delivered you and ransomed you with his precious blood.

Chapter 45: The Contemplative Life Restores the Image of the Trinity

   Even though God's mercy really does extend to you and
me and the whole human race, we must not let our trust in this

make us careless and willful in the course of our daily lives. We should be all the more anxious to please him, especially since we have been redeemed by our Lord's passion and can hope to regain that honor and joy that was lost by Adam's sin. Although we can never fully retrieve it here on earth, we should still desire to recover a semblance or likeness to that nobility so that our soul can be reformed, as it were, by means of grace to a shadow of the image of the Trinity that was originally bestowed upon us and that we shall fully possess in heaven. For a true contemplative life begins to experience here on earth that love and spiritual knowledge of God that will be fulfilled in the joys of heaven. It opens the eye of the soul and it can never be lost or taken away from us. Our Lord promised Mary Magdalene, who was a contemplative, that this was so when he said to her, *Maria optimam partem elegit, quae non auferatur ab ea*[24]: "Mary has chosen the better part (that is, the love of God in contemplation) because it can never be taken away from her."

I am not saying that you will be able to recover such a complete and perfect purity and innocence, knowledge and love of God as you had originally, or as you will have in the next world. Nor can you escape all the misery and pain of sin, nor, living as you are in a mortal body, will you be able to destroy and extinguish that false, trivial self-love. Nor can you flee all sensual sins or prevent them from continually springing up from your heart like water from a polluted well, unless they are stopped up by an ardent charity. But even though you cannot entirely eliminate it, I would like you to slake it somewhat and come as close as you can to purity of soul. For when our Lord led the children of Israel into the Promised Land, he promised them — and symbolically promised all Christians in them: *Omnis locus, quem calcaverit pes tuus tuum erit.*[25] This can be interpreted like this: "You will own as much of the Promised Land as you can tread with the feet of pure desire, that is, when you attain the bliss of heaven."

Chapter 46: The Centrality of Jesus in the Contemplative Life

Seek what you have lost in order to find it. I know that anybody who has an inner vision or even a glimpse of that nobility and spiritual beauty that was once natural to the soul and that he will receive by grace will certainly hate and despise all the joys, pleasures, and beauty of this world and regard it as a stinking corpse. He will never want to do anything by night or by day, but yearn, mourn, pray, and look for the means of recovering that original state once more, except when he is prevented by weakness and the basic needs of his body. But because you have not seen this fully, since the eye of your soul is still closed, I will tell you the word that sums up everything you seek, desire, and will find, because this word contains everything you have lost. The word is "Jesus." I don't simply mean the word "Jesus" that you find painted on the wall or inscribed in a book, which is formed by the lips to issue in sound from the mouth or produced by an intellectual activity in your heart. If that was all I meant, even a man who does not live in charity could find him! The reality that I am referring to when I say the name of "Jesus" is perfect goodness, eternal wisdom, love and sweetness — your happiness, your honor and everlasting joy, your God, your Lord and your Salvation.

If it happens, therefore, that you experience a great desire for Jesus in your heart, either by recalling the name of Jesus or by bringing any other word to mind during your prayers or in any other activity, which inspires a desire that is so great that it casts out, so to speak, all other thoughts and desire of the world and the flesh by force so that they cannot remain in your heart, then you are truly seeking your Lord Jesus. And when you experience such a longing for God or Jesus — it doesn't matter which — helped and comforted by a spiritual power that is so great it is transformed into love and devotion, spiritual delight and sweetness, light and knowledge so true that for a moment your mind is conscious of no created thing, feels no stirring of empty pride or evil passion — none of which can appear at this time — but is simply enclosed, at rest, soothed and anointed by Jesus, then you have found something of Jesus. Not him as he is in himself but a shadow of him, for the more you find him the more you are bound to long for him. Then you are truly looking for him and discovering him, whatever kind of prayer, meditation, or exercise brings you the greatest and most pure desire for him and gives you the most poignant experience of him. So if, as it were, you hear a voice in your mind asking what you have lost and what you are looking for, lift up the longing of your heart to the Lord Jesus Christ, son of blessed Mary, even though you are blind and can see nothing of his divinity. Tell him that he is the one you have lost, he whom you desire and nothing but him — no other joy, no other happiness in heaven or earth but him alone. But, even if you seem to experience him in devotion, in knowledge or by any other gift whatever, don't rest in this, as though you had completely found Jesus. Forget what you have already discovered and keep on yearning for Jesus more and more in order to find him still more perfectly. For you must understand that whatever your experience and however sublime it seems — yes! even if you are rapt into the third heaven with St. Paul — you have still not found Jesus as he is in his joy. However great your knowledge and experience of him, he himself exceeds it. And so if you want to find him as he truly is in the beatitude of his eternal love, never stop longing for him spiritually as long as you live.

Chapter 48: Be Like the Woman in the Gospel Parable

Be like the woman in the gospel of whom our Lord said, *Quae mulier habens drachmas decem, si perdideris unam nonne accendit lucernam, et everrit domum suam et quaerit diligenter donec inveniat eam? Et cum invenerit, convocat amicos suos, dicens: Congratulamini mihi, quia inveni drachmam, quam perdideram*[26]: "Is there a woman who loses a drachma, who will not light a lantern and turn her house upside down and look until she finds it?" This question clearly expects us to answer "No." When the woman has found her coin, she calls her friends to her and says to them, "Celebrate and sing with me, because I have found the drachma that I had lost." The drachma is Jesus, whom you have lost. If you want to find him, light a lantern that is the word of God, as David says, *Lucerna pedibus meis verbum tuum*[27]: "Lord, your word is a lamp to guard my feet." By this lamp, you are bound to see where he is and discover how to find him. And if you wish, you can light another lamp, that is, the reasoning power of your soul, for our Lord has also said, *Lucerna corporis tui est oculus tuus*[28]: "Your eye is the lamp of your body." In the same way it can be said that reason is the lamp of the soul, which enables it to see all the things of the spirit. You can find Jesus by means of this lantern, if you lift it from under the bushel, as our Lord has said, *Nemo accendit lucernam et posit eum sub modio, sed super candelabrum, etc.*[29]: "Nobody lights a lamp to put it under a bushel but upon a candlestick." That is to say, your reason should not be covered up with worldly affairs, trivial thoughts, and bodily passions but should always be rising above the things of the world as much as it can. If you do this you are bound to discover all the dust, filth, and tiny motes in your house (Why? because he is light); this can be interpreted thus: all the physical desire and fear in your soul. Not all, because as David says, *Delicta quis intelligit?*[30]: "Who can know all his shortcomings?" meaning that nobody can. And you must throw all such sins out of your heart and sweep your soul clean with the broom of the fear of God and wash it with water from your eyes.

In this way you are bound to find Jesus, your drachma. He is a drachma, a penny, and he is your inheritance. This drachma won't be found as easily as my description suggests. It is not a job for an hour or a day but for many days and years with toil and sweat of body and travail of the soul. And if you don't give up but search zealously, sorrow and sigh deeply, mourn ceaselessly and bend so low that water pours with pain and anguish from your eyes because you have lost Jesus, your drachma, eventually, when he sees fit, you will find your drachma, Jesus. And if you do find him in the way that I suggest (that is, if you are able to experience, with a pure conscience, the intimate and peaceful presence of that blessed man Jesus Christ), that is, a shadow or glimmering of him, you can if you wish call your friends to you and celebrate and sing because you have found Jesus, your drachma.

Chapter 51: The Livery of Christ

Prepare to be arrayed in the likeness of Christ, that is, in the humility and charity that are his livery, and he will know you intimately and show you his deepest secrets. Thus he himself said to his disciples, *Qui diligit me, diligetur a Patre meo, et manifestabo ei meipsum*[31]: "Whoever loves me will be loved by my Father, and I will show myself to him." There is no virtue or exercise that you can undertake that will make you like our Lord but humility and charity, for these two virtues are the special livery of God and specially pleasing to him. It certainly seems that this is so in the gospel, when our Lord speaks of humility: *Discite a me, quia mitis sum et humilis corde*[32]: "Learn from me," he says, "not to go barefoot or vanish into the desert to fast for forty days, nor to select your disciples, but learn humility from me, for I am meek and humble of heart." He also said this about charity: *Hoc est preceptum meum: ut diligatis invicem sicut dilexi vos. Item in hoc cognoscent homines quia discipuli mei estis, si dilectionem habueritis ad invicem*[33]: "This is my commandment: that you should love each other as I have loved you, for this is the way that people will recognize you as my disciples. Not because you work miracles or cast out devils or preach or teach; but that each of you loves each other in charity." If you want to be like him, you must have humility and charity. Charity consists in this: that you know how to love your fellow Christians.

Chapter 83: How a Contemplative Should Behave with Visitors

Now you will tell me that you cannot stop hearing about trivial or damaging things, because so many people — some worldly, some not — come to talk to you frequently and tell you about these worldly vanities.

To this my reply is that conversation with your fellow Christians is not particularly harmful but can even help you, provided that you use it wisely. This is the way to test the degree of charity you have toward your fellow Christians and see whether your love is great or small. Like everybody else, you have an obligation to love your fellow Christians, first in your heart, but also in your actions. You must give them such tokens of charity as can be reasonably demanded, insofar as you can and know how. Now, since you are not allowed to leave your convent to help your fellow Christians in works of charity because you are an enclosed nun, you are still bound to love them with all your heart and to show your visitors signs of love. And therefore be ready and willing to find out what the people who come to talk to you really want. You should do this whoever he is, whatever state of life he is in, even if you don't know who he is or why he has come. Don't be aloof or make him wait for a long time, but think how prompt and happy you would be if an angel came from heaven to talk to you like this. You should be just as prompt and graciously eager to talk to your fellow Christian when he comes to visit you. You don't know who he is, or why he has come, nor what need he has of you or you of him until you have made an attempt to find out. Even if you are at your prayers and spiritual exercises and are loath to break off because it seems wrong to leave God to talk to men instead, this doesn't seem the right attitude to me. If you were really aware of what you are about, you don't leave God but find him, possess him and see him in your neighbor as clearly as you do in prayer, but in a different way.

If you really had the power to love your neighbor, it should not hold you back if you talk to him directly. It seems to me essential to exercise your discretion in this matter. Ask anybody who comes to you, in a humble manner, what he wants. If he has come to tell you his troubles and to find comfort in your advice, listen willingly to him and let him say whatever he wants to ease his heart. When he has finished, comfort him as kindly and lovingly as you can and then quickly leave off. If he then lapses into idle chitchat or trivial gossip about other people's business, answer briefly and don't encourage him. He will soon get fed up and leave. If your visitor is another kind of person, like a man of the Church, who has come to instruct you, listen humbly and reverently to his directions and don't start giving him instruction! It is not your place to instruct a priest, unless he has need of you. If you don't find his conversation consoling, answer him briefly and he will soon take his leave. Or if somebody else arrives to give you alms, to hear you talk or to take instruction from you, speak kindly and humbly to them all. Don't reprove anybody for his failings: this is not your job unless he is a friend of yours and you know that he can take such a reproof. In short, talk as much as you think will help your neighbor, if he can bear it. Keep as quiet as possible about all other matters and in a little while you will find that this pressure from the outside world won't hurt your spiritual life. This is my advice, but by all means improve on it if you can.

Book 2. Chapter 5: The Reformation of Faith and the Reformation of Feeling

It is possible for us to reshape ourselves at least in part to the image of Christ, and we must undergo this reformation here on earth or we cannot be saved. But this reformation happens in two ways: in faith and in feeling. The first way — the reformation in faith alone — is the basic requirement for salvation; the second entitles us to a special reward in the joy of heaven. The first can be attained easily and quickly, but not the second, which can only be achieved by a long and intense spiritual effort. The first can be achieved with the experience of sin, because even though a man feels nothing within himself but sins, temptations, and carnal desire, yet despite this he can be reformed to the image of God in faith, provided that he does not choose to give in to sin. But the reformation of feeling expels all attraction to sin, fleshly impulses, and worldly desire; it allows no such flaws to tarnish the image of God in our souls. The first kind of reformation is only a beginning of spiritual progress and for people who live the active life. But the second is for people who are seeking perfection and contemplation. By the first reformation, the image of sin is not destroyed in us but we seem to remain wholly susceptible to it. But the second kind of reformation destroys our old consciousness of this sinful image within us and brings new feelings of grace into the soul through the activity of the Holy Spirit. The first reformation is good, and the second is better, but the third (which is the bliss of heaven) is without doubt the best of all. I will speak of all three reformations in turn.

Chapter 8: The Sacrament of Confession

The first kind of reformation is rooted in faith and not in felt experience because, as it is the very nature of faith to believe what you do not see, it is also to believe something that you cannot feel or experience. But a person whose soul is reformed by the sacrament of confession feels no different, either in body or in the hidden depths of his soul, from what he was before. He is just the same person as before. He experiences the same temptations to sin and the same corruption of the flesh; passions and desires rise up in his heart in the same old way. And yet he still has to believe that he has been reformed through grace to the image of God, even though he cannot feel this or see it. He may well feel sorrow for his sin and an inclination to turn away from it to adopt a pure way of life, if he receives the grace to do so and watches over himself. But he cannot see or feel that reformation of his soul, which has miraculously and imperceptibly put away that diabolical filth and assumed the beauty of an angel, through the hidden, gracious activity of our Lord God. He cannot see this but he has to believe it, and, if he believes it, his soul is reformed indeed.

Holy Church believes that when the sacrament of baptism is properly administered, a Jew, a Muslim, or a newborn child is reformed in spirit to the image of God through a hidden and imperceptible activity of the Holy Spirit, in spite of all the temptations of the flesh urging his body to sin, which he will feel just as strongly after his baptism as before. In just the same way when the sacrament of confession is humbly and properly received, the soul of a bad Christian who has been laden with mortal sin all his life is reformed imperceptibly through a hidden, gracious activity of the Holy Spirit. This works immediately, in a moment, and reforms the perverse soul in the twinkling of an eye, changing its state from one of filth to an inexpressible beauty. It changes a servant of the devil to a son of joy; it makes a prisoner of hell an heir of heavenly bliss — in spite of all the carnal longings of the old sinful man, which is his physical nature. For you must understand that the sacraments of baptism and confession do not have the power to prevent and destroy totally all the carnal lusts and the painful passions. Thus, the human soul never feels the sacraments rising up or working within him. If he did, then the soul would be fully reformed to the dignity of its original creation here on earth, but that cannot happen in this life.

But the power of the sacraments does purify the soul of all the sins it committed before and, if it leaves the body, they save it from hell. If the soul remains in the body, the sacramental grace enables it to withstand temptation and it also keeps it in a state of grace so that none of the carnal temptations or passions it feels, however severe, can injure it or separate it from God provided that the soul does not give in to them. This is what St. Paul meant when he said, *Nihil damnationis est iis qui sunt in Christo, qui non secundum carnem ambulant etc.*[34] We might translate thus: "Those souls who are reformed to the image of God in faith, through the sacraments of baptism and confession, will not be damned because of the experiences of the old sinful man, provided that they do not follow up these bodily temptations and translate them into deeds."

From Chapter 15: People in the World Disable Themselves from Reforming Their Souls

Now some people say: "I would like to love God and be a good person and renounce the love of the world if I could, but I don't have the grace to do it. If I had the same grace as a good person I should do the same as he, but because I don't have it, I can't and it isn't within my power. So I am excused." I reply to such people that what they say is true; they have no grace and therefore they still wallow in their sins and cannot rise above them. But this will be no help or no excuse with God because it is their own fault. They disable themselves in so many ways that the light of grace cannot illuminate them or find a home in their hearts. Some are so perverse that they will never have any peace or become good men because they know very well that to become good they have to give up the great pleasure they take in the world and their passion for earthly things. They don't want to do that because it seems so sweet that they would rather not forgo it. They also need to adopt penitential practices, like fasts, vigils, prayers, and other good deeds to discipline their flesh and to help them withdraw from carnal passion. They can't do that because it seems so difficult and frightening that they are wary and hate thinking about it. That is why they still live in their sins, like cowards and poor inadequates.

Chapter 17: The Reformation of Faith and of
Feeling Takes a Long Time

As I explained earlier, the initial reformation of faith is
achieved easily. Next comes the reformation of faith *and* feeling, however, and this cannot be achieved so easily but only
by means of a sustained effort and much hard work. For the
reformation in faith is common to all the elect, even if they are
only on the lowest rung of charity. But the reformation of
feeling is only for those who have arrived at the state of
perfection, and that cannot be achieved all at once, even
though it is possible for a soul to attain it with a great deal of
grace and much spiritual effort. First, he is healed of his
spiritual sickness when his bitter passions, his physical lust,
and old emotions are burned out with the fire of love and the
light of the spirit. Then a soul comes close to perfection and to
the reformation of feeling.

A physical illness brings a man close to death, and even
when he takes a medicine that cures him and saves his life he
cannot get up all at once and go to work like a healthy
person. His weak body holds him down and he has to rest
for a long time and keep himself in good health with medicine, good food, and the advice of his doctor until he makes a
full recovery. In the same way in the spiritual life, a person
who is close to the death of his soul because of his sins may
be restored to life with the medicine of the sacrament of
confession, but he is not immediately healed of all his passions, his physical desires, nor is he ready for contemplation
all at once. He needs to rest awhile, take good care of
himself, and adopt a rule of life that will help him to recover
his full spiritual health. He is bound to be weak for a long
time until he is completely cured. Nevertheless, if he takes
the medicines of a good doctor and uses them at the proper
time and in the correct amounts and with discretion, he must

be restored to his full spiritual health quite soon and will arrive at the reformation of feeling.

For the reformation of faith is the lowest state of all God's elect: they cannot be lower than that. But the reformation of feeling is the highest state that a soul can attain in this life. But it cannot suddenly jump from the lowest to the highest rung, any more than a man who wants to climb a high ladder and puts his foot on the first rung can fly up to the top rung in one step. He has to proceed in the usual way, step by step, until he reaches the top. It is just the same in the spiritual life. Nobody becomes a champion overnight by means of grace, but a soul can arrive at the highest state through a sustained discipline and skillful exercise, especially when God helps or instructs a poor soul with grace within him, for without that special help and interior instruction, nobody can succeed.

From Chapter 21: The Heavenly Jerusalem

But because you long to have a special exercise to bring you closer to that supreme reformation, I will tell you what I think is the quickest and most direct method I know, with the grace of our Lord Jesus Christ. I am going to explain it by taking the *exemplum* of a good pilgrim, like this:

There was once a man who wanted to go to Jerusalem and, because he did not know the way, he went to another man who he hoped did, and asked the way to the city. This person told him that he would not be able to reach his destination without great distress and torment, for it is a long journey, there is great danger from thieves and bandits and many other obstacles that a man has to encounter on the road. It also appeared that there were several different routes that led to Jerusalem, but that people were continually killed and robbed and never reached the place they sighed for. But there was one road that he was ready to vouch for: anybody who opted for it and stuck to it would certainly reach the city of Jerusalem and would never lose his life, nor be killed nor die by an accident. He would inevitably be robbed and frequently be beaten up and suffer a great deal of distress during his journey, but he would save his life.

Then the pilgrim said: "If it is true that my life will be safe and I shall reach the place I long for, I don't care what I have to suffer on the way, so tell me whatever you want and I promise to do what you say." The other man replied like this: "Look," he said, "I am putting you on the right path. This is the road and you must abide by the instructions I give you. If you hear or see any obstacle during your journey, don't trifle with it and don't be afraid of it but persevere down this road and remember that you are aiming at Jerusalem. That is what you long for, that is what you covet and nothing else. If somebody robs you and strips you of your clothes, beats you, insults you and treats you with contempt, don't fight with him if you want to save your life. Put up with the injury you have received and keep going as though nothing had happened or you might suffer more harm. Again, if people attempt to hold you up by telling you stories or by stuffing your head with lies to tempt you to the fleshpots and to abandon your pilgrimage, stop your ears and refuse to answer, saying only that you want to get to Jerusalem. If people offer you gifts and promise you riches in this world, take no notice of them: keep Jerusalem continually in your mind and if you stick to this road and do what I have told you, you will not be slain but you are bound to reach the place you desire."

Now for our purpose, we can say that in the spiritual life "Jerusalem" means the vision of peace and symbolizes contemplation in the perfect love of God. For contemplation is simply the vision of Jesus who is true peace. So if you long to reach this blessed vision of true peace and become a real pilgrim *en route* to Jerusalem, I can direct you, even though it is true that I have never been there myself. The beginning of this highway on which you walk is the reformation of faith: its roots are fixed humbly in the faith and the laws of Holy Church. You can be perfectly confident that, even if you have sinned in your past life, you have now been reformed by the sacrament of confession, according to the laws of Holy Church. You are on the right road. Now then, since that is so, if you want your journey to be quick and successful, you must keep these two things in mind: humility and love. That is, you should say: "I am nothing, I have nothing and I long for nothing but one thing." You must keep the meaning of these words in sight and make this a continuous habit of your soul, even if you don't have the actual words themselves fixed in your mind — that is not necessary. Humility says: "I am nothing; I have nothing." Love says: "I desire nothing but one thing and that is Jesus." These two strings, tied securely to the remembrance of Jesus, create a beautiful harmony on the harp of your soul when they are skillfully touched by the finger of reason. For the deeper the note you strike on the first string, the higher will be your note on the other. The more humbly you consider yourself and assess your gifts, the more you long and lovingly yearn to have Jesus. I am not simply talking about the humility that a soul experiences when he looks at his own sins, frailties, and miseries in this life or at the excellent example he has from his neighbor for, though this humility is fitting and a useful medicine, it is, nevertheless, crude and earth-based in its vision, not pure, sweet, and lovely. But I really mean that humility a soul experiences through grace when it gazes at the eternal being and astonishing goodness of Jesus. If you can't see it yet with the eye of your soul, then believe in it. For by gazing at his essence either with perfect faith or a real perception, you are bound not merely to consider yourself the most pitiable creature in existence, but also to realize that you are essentially nothing — even if you had never committed a single sin. Now that is a beautiful humility, for, compared with Jesus, who is in truth all things, you are nothing at all. Also consider that you really possess nothing, but that you are like a jug that is always empty, as though you contained nothing in yourself. For no matter how many good works you perform, external or interior, unless you truly possess and feel that you have acquired the love of Jesus, you really have nothing at all, for the only thing that can really fill the soul up is that precious liquid — nothing else will do.

Because this love is the only precious and valuable reality, you ought, therefore, to consider what you have and what you do as no true support without the vision and love of Jesus. Put everything else behind you and forget all about it in order to possess the thing that is best of all.

Just as a good pilgrim on the road to Jerusalem leaves his house, his land, his wife and child behind and makes himself poor, stripped of everything he owns so that he can travel light, so if you want to be a spiritual pilgrim, you must strip yourself naked of everything you own — good deeds as well as bad — and cast them all behind you. Then you will become so poor in your own estimation of yourself that you will not willingly rely on any of your achievements. Instead you long ceaselessly for the grace of more love and constantly seek the spiritual presence of Jesus. In order to do this, you must keep your heart set wholly and completely on Jerusalem, your destination, and cast everything else from your mind. That means that you must set your heart wholly and completely on the love of Jesus so that you desire nothing else and keep your mind fixed on the spiritual vision of himself that he longs to show you. This was the sole purpose of your creation and redemption; it is your beginning, your end, your joy and your bliss. And therefore it doesn't matter how many things you possess, how rich you are in corporal or spiritual good works; unless you know and feel that you have that love you should consider that you have nothing at all. Engrave this observation in your heart and cleave to it seriously and then it will save you from the dangers of your journey: you will not perish and it will save you from thieves and bandits, which is what I call unclean spirits; even if they strip you and beat you up with many temptations, your life will always be safe. And soon, if you do what I tell you, you are bound to come through all the dangers and reach the city of Jerusalem.

From Chapter 24: The Dark Night

The everlasting love of Jesus is true day and blessed night. For God is a love and light that will last forever and so somebody who loves him always lives in this light, as St. John said: *Qui diliget Deum manet in lumine*[35]: "He who loves God lives entirely in light." Such a man realizes that the love of this world is false and unreliable and so he will forsake it and seek the love of God instead. He cannot experience this love immediately but has to stay for a while in the night, because he cannot suddenly pass from one light to another, that is, from the love of the world to the perfect love of God. This night is simply a rejection and withdrawal on the part of the soul from earthly things. The soul is inspired by a great desire and yearning to love, see, and experience Jesus and spiritual reality. This withdrawal is the night: for just as night is dark, and so all physical creatures are hidden and all bodily activities suspended, so too a man who sets himself to think about Christ and only desire his love, energetically hides his mind from the empty consideration of all earthly creatures and withdraws his affections from carnal enjoyment. He wants his mind to be free instead of fixed, and does not want his emo-

tions to be fettered, pained, or distressed about something
even more base and in a worse state than he is himself. If he
can do this he enters into the night because he is in darkness.

But this is a good night and the darkness is filled with
light, for it blocks out the false love of the world and comes
close to the true day. And indeed, the darker this night, the
closer it is to the true day of the love of Jesus. For the more
a soul is hidden from the noise and din of carnal emotions
and impure thoughts by his desire for God, the closer it is to
the experience of the light of his love, for God is right there.
It seems that this is what the prophet meant when he said:
Cum in tenebris sedeo, Dominus lux mea est,[36] which means that
when I sit in the darkness our Lord is my light. This can be
interpreted thus: when my soul is hidden from every motion
of sin, as though it were asleep, then our Lord is my light, for
it is then that he graciously approaches me to show me his
light.

Sometimes this night is painful and sometimes easy and
comfortable. It is painful at first when a man is still very
impure and not used to this darkness, even though he wants it.
He sets his mind on God and directs all his desire to Him as
far as he can, and he does not want to experience or think
about anything but him. But because this does not come easily
to him, it is painful, since he is more used to sins of the world
and carnal passions, more at home with the things of this
world. His bodily activities press so urgently on him, beat him
so thoroughly and drag him down to their level, that he cannot
hide from them as he would like. And so the darkness is
painful to him, especially when he is not touched by an
abundance of grace. But if it is like this for you, don't be too
depressed or struggle too much as if you could eject these
things from your mind by an act of will. That is impossible.
Instead, wait for grace; don't fight against your suffering and
don't put too much strain upon yourself. If you can, draw

your desire and your spiritual gaze toward Jesus slyly, as if you did not want to make a headlong charge!

Understand this: when you want to desire Jesus and think about him alone and yet find you cannot do it because of the throng of worldly thoughts that harry you, you are not really outside the false day. You are on the threshold of the darkness but not yet at rest because of your own inexperience, lack of skill, and impurity. So resort frequently to the darkness and gradually, by means of grace, it is bound to become easier and more peaceful. When that happens, your soul has become so free, powerful, and integrated by the power of grace that it does not want to think of anything and, indeed, is able to think of nothing without any hindrance from the things of this world. Then the soul is in a good darkness.

This is all I mean: by means of grace, a soul can be integrated and stand freely and entirely at peace within itself. It is not driven against its will or dragged down by force to think about sin or find pleasure or affection for any empty earthly thing. The soul thinks of nothing because it thinks of no earthly thing with attachment. This is a rich nothing. And this nothing and this night becomes a great rest for the soul that desires the love of Jesus. The soul may not think about any earthly thing, but it is very keen to think about God.

What is it that creates such a darkness? Nothing, indeed, but a gracious desire to have the love of Jesus. For the desire and longing that a soul has at this time to love God, see him, and possess him drives all worldly vanities and earthly affections from his heart. It integrates the powers of the soul and takes it over, so that its only thought is how it can come to love God. This is what brings it to that rich nothing. And really it is not all darkness and nothingness when it thinks like this. There may be an absence of false light but not an absence of true love. For Jesus, who is both love and light, is in this darkness, whether it is painful or peaceful. He is present in the soul as it labors in its desire and longing for the light but not yet in the peace of love, not yet revealing his light. That is why it is called night and darkness, because the soul has been hidden from the false light of the world and has not yet fully experienced the light. It is waiting instead for that blessed love of the God it longs for.

So if you want to know whether you are in this secure darkness or not, you can make this test and need look no further. When you feel that your intention and will are wholly fixed on the desire for God and think only of him, you can, so to speak, ask yourself within your own mind whether you want to have or enjoy anything in this life with the five senses of your body. Then, if your eye starts up and answers, "I don't want to see anything"; and then your ear says, "I don't want to hear anything at all"; and your mouth says, "There is absolutely nothing I want to taste and I don't want to say anything at all about the things of this world"; and your nose says, "There is absolutely nothing I want to smell"; and your body, "There is nothing I would feel," and, finally, your heart says, "I don't want to think about earthly things or physical activities; I don't want my affections to be engaged physically with any creature but only with God and if I can I would like to be directed only toward God," then you have begun to enter this darkness, if they all answer you like this — and, if you are touched by grace, it is very readily done. For though you may still feel and see glimmerings and premonitions of empty thoughts and the pressure of physical affection, you are still in this profitable darkness as long as your thought remains unattached to them. Such vain fantasies that fall into the heart without permission disturb this darkness and distress the soul a little, because it would like to be hidden from them and this is beyond its power. But they do not cancel out the benefit of this darkness and in this way the soul is bound to reach the darkness of rest. The darkness becomes restful when the soul is hidden for a while from the painful experience of all empty thoughts like this and only finds rest in the desire and longing for Jesus with a spiritual vision of him that I will explain later. This experience in its entirety only lasts for a while, but however brief it is, there is nothing more beneficial.

From Chapter 27: Death to Self

This darkness is a death to the world; it is the only gate to contemplation and the reformation of feeling. There may be various other methods and exercises that lead souls toward contemplation: these are all designed to suit different temperaments and the different states of life in which men find themselves, religious or secular. But for all that, there is only one gate. Whatever discipline he has used, no soul has attained the reformation of feeling or full contemplation unless it has brought him to this knowledge and humble perception of himself, which means that self has been put to death, that his love for the world is also dead, and that he sometimes feels that he sits in that peaceful darkness which hides him from the vanity of the world and makes him see himself as he really is. If not, he is very far from his goal. If he wants to enter by any other gate, he is just a thief and a gate-crasher and he will be thrown out because he is unworthy. But somebody who can reduce himself to nothing, by the grace of humility, and dies in this way stands at the gate because he is dead to the world and alive to God. St. Paul speaks of a person like this when he says, *Mortui enim estis, et vita vestra abscondita est cum Christo in Deo*[37]: "You are 'dead,' that means that those of you who have forsaken all love for the world for the love of God are dead to the world, but your life is hidden from worldly men, just as Christ is alive and hidden in his divinity from the love and sight of the people who love this world."

Our Lord himself revealed this in the gospel, when he said, *Omnis qui reliquerit patrem aut matrem, fratrem aut sororem propter me, centulum accipiet, et vitam aeternam possidebit*[38]: "Every man that for my sake leaves father or mother, sister or brother or any earthly good will have a hundredfold in this life and the bliss of heaven in the next world." The hundredfold that a soul will possess if it abandons the world is simply the reward of this light-filled darkness, which I call the gate of contemplation. For anyone who is in this darkness and is hidden, through grace, from the vanity of this world, does not long for its rewards, does not seek them, is not troubled by them, takes no notice of them, does not love them and so he has a hundred times more than the King or somebody who longs for worldly prosperity. Somebody who longs only for Jesus has a hundredfold, because he has more rest, more peace of heart, more true love and spiritual pleasure in one day than somebody who loves the world and has all the wealth he wants enjoys in a whole lifetime.

So this is a good darkness and a rich nothing, which brings the soul so much spiritual rest and so great a quiet. I think that this is what David was referring to when he said, *Ad Nihilum redactus sum, et nescivi.*[39] That is, "I was reduced to nothing and I did not know it." This means, the grace of our Lord Jesus Christ sent into my heart has slain and reduced to nothing all my love of the world and I do not know how. For it was not through any effort or act of will of my own that I no longer have this love but through the grace of our Lord Jesus. And so it seems to me that anyone who wishes to receive the light of grace and feel abundantly the love of Jesus in his soul must forsake all false light of earthly love and live in this darkness. And for all that, if he is afraid at first to live there, let him not turn back to the love of the world but let him endure a while and put all his hope and trust in Jesus and it will not be long before he receives some spiritual light. This is what the prophet advises: *Qui ambulavit in tenebris, et non est lumen ei, speret in Domino, et innitatur super Deum suum.*[40] By the words "Whoever goes in darkness and has no light," he means: whoever wants to hide himself from the love of the world and does not easily feel the light of spiritual love. Such a person must not despair or turn back to the world, but "hope in our Lord and lean upon him." The prophet means that he should trust in God, cling to him with all his heart, and wait for a while and he will certainly have light.

It is like a man who has been in the sun for a long time and then walks into a house where there is no sunlight. At first he is blind, so to speak, and sees absolutely nothing. But if he will wait awhile, he will soon be able to look about him and see first big things, then small things and finally everything in the house. It is just the same in the spiritual life. Someone who abandons the life of the world and enters his own conscience finds that at first it is rather dark and he cannot see. But if he stands still and perseveres in frequent prayer, thinking himself into the love of Jesus, he will afterward be able to see great and small things that he did not perceive at first. It seems that the prophet promised this when he said: *Orietur in tenebris lux tua, et tenebrae tuae erunt sicut meridies. Et requiem dabit Dominus Deus tuus, et implebit animam tuam splendoribus*[41]: "Light shall spring to thee in darkness," which means, you who have truly forsaken the light of all worldly love and hide your thoughts in this darkness will find that the light of blessed love and the spiritual knowledge of God will spring to thee. "And thy darkness shall be like the noontide." That means, the darkness of your original desire and toil and your blind faith in God will turn into clear knowledge and certainty of love. "And thy Lord God shall give you light." That means, your carnal desires, your painful fears and doubts and the evil spirits who have incessantly troubled you until now shall all become weak and their great power will grow less. You will become so strong that they will not harm you for you will be hidden from them and at rest. "And then our Lord Jesus will fill thy soul with his brightness." That means, when you have been brought into this spiritual rest, you will incline to God more easily and do nothing but love him. Then with beams of spiritual light he will satisfy all the powers of your soul. Don't be surprised if I call the rejection of worldly love a darkness. The prophet calls it this too when he says to a soul: *Intra in tenebris tuas, filia Chaldaeorum*[42]: "Go into thy darkness, O daughter of Chaldea," which means, You, my soul, who in your love for the world are a daughter of Chaldea, forsake it and enter your darkness.

Chapter 31: The Reformation of Feeling

I have now told you a little about the reformation of faith and I have also touched briefly on the way to progress from that first reformation to the higher state of the reformation of feeling. When I spoke of these matters, I did not mean to subject the work of God to my own theories, as though I were saying: this is the way that God works in a soul and no other way will do! No, indeed, I didn't mean that at all: I was merely describing my own simple observations of the way that our Lord Jesus had worked in other souls. But I expect that he also works in quite different ways that exceed my understanding and observation. Nevertheless, whether he works this way or that, in different exercises that take a long or a short time, with great or little effort, provided that it is all directed toward one end — the perfect love of God — then that is quite good enough. For if he wants to give one soul the full grace of contemplation in a single day without any trouble at all — as he can do very easily — that is just as beneficial to the soul as if it had been put to the test, made to suffer, mortified, and purified for twenty years. This is the way you should understand what I have told you, namely, that I am speaking about these matters as I see them. Now, by the grace of our Lord Jesus, I am going to speak a little more clearly about the reformation of feeling, as I see it. I am going to describe what it is, how it is achieved, and what spiritual experiences the soul receives.

But first of all, in order that you do not interpret this description as a fake or a fantasy, I am going to base it on St. Paul's words, when he says, *Nolite conformari huic saeculo, sed reformamini in novitate sensus vestri,*[43] which can be roughly translated: "You who are reformed through grace in faith, do not conform any more to the customs of this world in pride, covetousness and other sins but be transformed in a new kind of feeling." Look, here you can see that St. Paul speaks of this reformation of feeling and he describes this new feeling elsewhere: *Ut impleamini in agnitione voluntatis ejus, in omni intellectu et sapientia spiritali.*[44] That is: "We pray God that you may be fulfilled in the knowledge of God's will, in all understanding and all kinds of spiritual wisdom." This is the reformation of feeling. For you must understand that the soul has two kinds of feeling: one which is beyond the five senses of our body and another that is experienced within the spiritual senses, which are more correctly called the powers of the soul: memory, reason, and will. When, by means of grace, these powers are completely filled with the understanding of God's will and spiritual wisdom, the soul has new feelings, informed by grace. St. Paul shows this when he says, *Renovamini spiritu mentis vestrae, et induite novum hominem, qui secundum Deum creatus est in justitia, sanctitate, et veritate*[45]: "Be ye renewed in the spirit of your soul." That means, you must be transformed not by physical experience or in your imagination, but in the higher part of your reason. "And clothe yourself in the new man that is formed in righteousness, in the image of God."

Your reason, which is really the image of God through the grace of the Holy Spirit, must be clothed in a new kind of truthfulness, holiness, and righteousness and then it is re-formed in feeling. For when the soul has a perfect knowledge of God, it is reformed. As St. Paul says, *Espoliantes veterem hominem cum actibus suis; induite novum, qui renovatur in agnitione Dei, secundum imaginem ejus qui creavit eum.*[46] "Spoil yourself of the old man" means, cast from you the love of the world and all worldly preconceptions. "And clothe yourself in the new man": that means you must be renewed in the knowledge of God in the image of him who created you.

You can understand by these words that St. Paul wanted men's souls reformed in the perfect knowledge of God, for that is the new feeling that he usually describes. And, there-fore, basing myself on him, I must speak more clearly about this reformation, as far as God gives me grace. For there are two ways of knowing God. One is chiefly by means of the imagination, without much understanding. This knowledge is the start of the life of grace and profitable to those elect souls who know God and love him in a human rather than in a spiritual way, with human emotions, and who see him in physical ways as I described earlier. This knowledge is good, and it has been compared to milk by means of which they are tenderly nourished like children until they are ready to sit at their father's table and take the whole loaf from his hand. The other kind of knowledge is chiefly experienced by the intel-ligence when it has been consoled and enlightened by the Holy Spirit without much help from the imagination, its handmaid, who serves the understanding when it is necessary. This kind of knowledge is the whole loaf, meat for perfect souls, and it is the reformation of feeling.

Chapter 32: How We Know God

A soul who is called from the love of the world and is then corrected and put to the test, mortified and purified in the way I have described, is reformed in feeling by our Lord Jesus in his merciful goodness when he chooses to do so. He opens the inner eyes of the soul when he enlightens the reason by touching and shining his blessed light upon it so that it can see and know him. This does not happen completely or all at once but gradually at different times as the soul is able to bear it. He does not see *what* God is, for no created thing in heaven and earth can do that; neither does he see him *as* he is, for that vision is reserved for the bliss of heaven. But he sees *that* he is: a changeless being, a sovereign power, a sovereign truth, a blessed life, an endless happiness. The soul sees this and much more besides, not blindly, bleakly, and abstractly like a scholar with his natural learning and unaided reason, but the soul sees *that* God exists in his understanding, which is comforted and enlightened by the gift of the Holy Spirit with a marvelous reverence, a hidden and burning love, a spiritual savor and a heavenly delight. He sees more purely and completely than it is possible to describe in writing or speech.

Even though this vision may be brief and incomplete, it is so precious and powerful that it draws and ravishes the emotions of the soul from all thought and remembrance of things here below. The soul wishes that it were possible to stay in this state forever. On this vision and knowledge, the soul bases all its interior activity and all its affections. For then the soul fears God as Truth, is astonished by him as Power, and loves him as Goodness. This vision and knowledge of Jesus, together with the blessed love that comes with it, can be described as the soul's "reformation in faith and in feeling," which I am trying to explain to you. It is a reformation in faith because, compared with the full knowledge that will be ours in heaven, it is still obscure. For then we shall not only see *that* he is, but we shall also see him *as* he is. As St. John says, *Tunc videbimus eum sicuti est,*[47] that is, "Then we shall see him as he is." But it is a reformation of feeling, too, compared with the blind knowledge of a soul that is based on faith alone. For this soul knows something about the divine nature of Jesus by means of the grace-inspired vision, but the man reformed only in faith has no such knowledge but only believes that it is true.

But to help you to understand me better, I will show you the three ways by which a soul is reformed, using the example of three men standing in the sunlight. One is blind, another is able to see but his eyes are closed, and the third is able to look around him with no impediment.

The blind man has no way of knowing that he is standing in the sunlight, but he believes it if a reliable person tells him so. And he symbolizes a soul that is only reformed in faith, that believes in God as Holy Church teaches and does not know any more. This reformation is sufficient for salvation.

The next man sees some sunlight but he does not see clearly what it is like, because his eyelids stop him. But he can see a great light glimmering through his eyelids and this man symbolizes a soul who is reformed in faith and feeling and is, therefore, a contemplative. Because he sees a glimpse of the divinity of Christ by means of grace, he does not see clearly or fully because of his eyelids, that is, his physical nature, which is still a wall between his natural state and the nature of Jesus, our God. But once he has been touched by grace he can see through this wall that Jesus is God and Jesus is sovereign goodness, sovereign being, and a blessed life and that all goodness is derived from him. The soul sees this by means of grace, despite its bodily nature, and the purer and more refined the soul becomes and the more it leaves our fleshly nature behind, the stronger its love for the divinity of Jesus. This is such a powerful vision that even if nobody else in the world believed in Jesus or loved him this soul would never stop believing in him or loving him. He sees it so clearly that he finds it impossible not to believe it.

The third man, who enjoys the full light of the sun, does not need to believe because he sees it fully. And he symbolizes that truly blessed soul who gazes openly on the face of Jesus in the bliss of heaven, without the wall of his body and of sin obstructing his vision. There is no faith here and so this soul is completely reformed in feeling.

In this earthly life no soul can climb above the second kind of reformation, for this higher state is the state of perfection and means that we are on the threshold of heaven. The souls who are in this state are not all alike, however. Some have the experience only partially, briefly, and infrequently; others have it very clearly and for a long time, having received abundant grace, yet they all have the gift of contemplation. A soul does not attain to a perfect vision of Jesus all at once. At first he sees only a little and afterward his vision develops and becomes clearer and as long as it lives in this world, its knowledge of Jesus can increase. Indeed, I don't know what more a soul who has had a glimpse of this knowledge can expect but that he must leave all things entirely behind, set them all at nought, and attend only to this contemplation, in order to have a more perfect vision and love of Jesus, in whom the whole blessed Trinity is comprised.

As I understand it, this way of knowing Jesus must be the opening of the heavens to the eye of a pure soul, which the holy men describe. This does not mean, as some people think, that when the heavens are opened the soul is able to see through the skies and above the firmament in his imagination at the way our Lord Jesus sits in his glory, bathed in a physical light as great as a hundred suns. No, it is not at all like that. However exalted such a vision might be, nobody really sees the spiritual heavens. The more somebody struggles to have a vision of Jesus our God sitting beyond the sun with an effort of his imagination, the lower he falls. Nevertheless, this kind of vision is permitted to simple souls who know no other way of looking for the God whom nobody can see.

From Chapter 34: God Himself Is the Cause of a Soul's Knowledge

Now, because the knowledge of God is the soul's happiness and final destination, you must be wondering why I said earlier that a soul must desire nothing but the love of God alone and did not mention this vision or say that a soul should desire it.

I will reply to your question thus: the vision of Jesus does not constitute the entire happiness of the soul, not because it is inadequate in itself but because we are only truly satisfied by the holy love that follows this vision. Because love derives from knowledge and not knowledge from love, however, it is said that the happiness of the soul consists principally in the knowledge, vision, and love of God combined, and that the more he is known the more he is loved. The reason I told you to desire love alone is that without it we will never experience either the knowledge of God or his harsh love that is its consequence. Love is the means whereby a soul attains this vision and knowledge, and that love is not the love of God that a soul possesses in its own right, but the love that our Lord has for a sinful soul that cannot love him properly. Divine love is the means by which a soul arrives at such knowledge and the love that follows from it. I must now explain more clearly.

Holy writers tell us — and it is true — that there are two kinds of spiritual love: uncreated and created love. Uncreated love is God himself, the third person of the Trinity — that is, the Holy Spirit. He is Love that has neither been created nor

made, as St. John says, *Deus dilectio est* [48]: "God is Love," and
that means the Holy Spirit. Created love is that inclination in
the soul toward the vision and knowledge of the Truth — that
is, God alone — which has been created by the Holy Spirit,
inspired and rooted in him. This love is called created because
it has been made by the Holy Spirit. But this love is not God
himself, because it has been created, but it is the love the soul
experiences when it sees Jesus and reaches out for him alone.
Now you can see that created love is the means whereby a
soul reaches the spiritual vision of Jesus, as some people
imagine that they love God so ardently — apparently by
means of their own effort — that they think that they deserve
to enjoy the spiritual knowledge of him. No, this is not the
case. It is Uncreated Love — that is, God himself, who is the
ground of this knowledge. For a poor blind soul is so far from
the pure vision and holy experience of love, because of sin and
the weakness of our human nature, that it could never attain it
without the eternal power of God's love. But then, it is because he loves us so much that he gives us his love — that is,
the Holy Spirit. He is both giver and gift, and by means of that
gift he enables us to know and love him.

Look, this is the love I mean: you should only covet and
desire this Uncreated Love which is the Holy Spirit. For
nothing less than this divine gift, this divine reality will bring
us to the holy vision of Jesus. And so we must yearn for this
gift of love with all our hearts and beg Jesus for this alone,
praying that out of the immensity of his blessed love he will
touch our hearts with his invisible light, with knowledge of
him, and bestow this holy love upon us, so that we may love
him with exactly the same love as he loves us. As St. John
says, *Nos diligamus Deum, quoniam ipse prior dilexit nos* [49]: "We
love God now because he loved us first." He loved us deeply
when he created us in his image, but he loved us even more
when he ransomed us by voluntarily accepting death in his

humanity and rescued us from the power of the enemy and the pains of hell. But he loves us most of all when he gives us the gift of the Holy Spirit — that is, Love — by means of whom we know him and love him and know for certain that we are his sons and among the elect who will be saved. Through this last act of love we are bound to him more closely than through any other act of love toward us, either in our creation or redemption. Because, even though he had created and redeemed us, what use would our creation and continued existence be to us if he had not also saved us? None at all.

And so it seems to me that the greatest sign of love he has shown us is this: that he gives himself in his divinity to our souls. He gave himself to us in his humanity first of all when he redeemed us by offering himself to the Father of heaven on the altar of the Cross. This was a beautiful gift and a great sign of love. But when he gives himself spiritually to our souls in his divinity in order to save us and enables us to know him and to love him, then he loves us most of all. Because he then gives himself to us: he cannot give us more than that, and anything less would not satisfy us. And it is for this reason that the redemption of a sinful soul through the forgiveness of sins is ascribed to the Holy Spirit and said to be chiefly his work. For the Holy Spirit is Love, and our Lord Jesus shows a soul his love most of all when he redeems it by ridding it of sin and uniting it to himself. That is the best thing he can do for a soul, and so it is attributed to the Holy Spirit.

The creation of a soul is attributed to the Father because of his surpassing Power and might that is shown in this creation. Its salvation is imputed and attributed to the son, because of the surpassing determination and wisdom that he showed in his humanity. He overcame the enemy chiefly by his wisdom and not through his strength. But the redemption and complete salvation of the soul by means of the forgiveness of sins is attributed to the third person, the Holy Spirit. For it is through the gift of the Spirit that Jesus shows his great love for the human soul, and this gift demands that we love him in return. We share the gift of creation with all the irrational beings, because he created them from nothing, just as he created us. Similarly, the gift of salvation is common to us and to all intelligent souls — even to Jews, Muslims, and bad Christians — because Jesus died for all souls alike and, if they wish to take advantage of it, he has redeemed all of them. He has paid a sufficient ransom for everybody, even though not everybody is willing to accept it. This was the work of divine Wisdom rather than of divine Love. But the redemption and sanctification of our souls by means of the gift of the Holy Spirit is solely the work of Love. It is not common to everybody but is a special gift for the elect alone, the greatest work of God's love for those of us who have been chosen to be his children.

This is the love of God that I urged you to covet and desire because it is God himself and the Holy Spirit. When this uncreated love is bestowed upon us, it activates all that is good in our soul and all that yearns for goodness. It is a Love that loves us before we love him. First, it cleanses us of sin, and makes us love God, strengthens our will to resist all sin in the future and inspires us to try to acquire all the virtues by means of disciplines of body and soul. It also inspires us to abandon the love of this world and any pleasure we take in it. It guards us from the evil temptations of the devil and forces us to stop being anxious, to stop pursuing the empty things of this world and dealing with worldly people. Such are the effects of the Uncreated Love of God when he gives himself to us. All we do is yield and surrender to him. Our main contribution is to submit willingly to his gracious activity within us, but even this goodwill is not an achievement of our own. It is of his making, so it seems to me that it is God who performs anything that is worth doing but that we fail to take advantage of it. This is not all he does for us: after bestowing his love upon us he does still more. He opens the eye of the soul and shows it the wondrous vision of Jesus, giving it, by slow degrees, such knowledge of him that the soul can bear.

Once the soul begins to know Jesus spiritually and to love him ardently, it has a glimpse of his holy divinity, sees how he is everything and does everything, and that all the good deeds and thoughts ever performed derive from him alone. For he is peerless Power, peerless Truth, and peerless Goodness. And so every good deed comes from him and through him and from him alone. No one but he should receive the honor and thanks for such good works. For, though man pathetically tries to steal this honor from him for a while here below, on the Last Day it will appear that in reality Jesus did everything and that man did nothing by his own powers. On that day, everybody who has stolen God's honor from him in this way without being reconciled to him during this life will be condemned to eternal death and Jesus will be glorified and thanked by all the blessed for his marvelous achievements.

IV

Dame Julian of Norwich

ulian of Norwich had an entirely different religious experience from the other writers we have considered in this book. She did not discover a numinous cloud of ignorance or an impenetrable darkness between herself and God; her apprehension of the divine did not end in silence, but in an eloquent message for her contemporaries. She calls her experiences "revelations" and is, perhaps, more like a prophet who brings a message of God to mankind than a mystic. Julian, of course, would not have described herself as a prophet, because like all monotheists at this date, she believed that God's revelation was complete and that the day of prophecy was therefore over. Yet it remains true that Julian's experience can be fruitfully compared to that of the prophets of Israel, for example, or to that of Muhammad, the prophet of Islam.

Julian was the latest of our four mystics. She was born in about 1342 and was still alive in 1416. She was an anchoress, one of the many recluses of the period who shut herself away from the world to pray in solitude: we can still see the foundations of her anchorage next to the church that is now called St.

Julian's in Norwich. Anchoresses were believed to confer
great spiritual benefits on a neighborhood, and all big towns
liked to have one. The people also valued the spiritual counsel
that the recluse would provide. She generally lived in a room
next to the church, which had a window in the wall through
which she could watch the Mass and receive the sacraments.
The anchoress would be interred in this room in an impressive
if rather disturbing ceremony during a Mass for the Dead.
She would publicly don her religious habit and walk into the
cell as into her grave, while the presiding bishop sprinkled
ashes in her wake. Henceforth, like St. Paul, she was dead to
the world and alive only to God. But it would be a mistake to
imagine that the anchorage was a tiny, smelly little room, as it
is sometimes depicted. It was usually a suite of rooms with a
garden, rather like a ground-floor flat. Some anchoresses
lived together in adjacent apartments and nearly all had servants. An anchoress had to be a woman of means or she would
become a drain on the community. We know that Julian had
at least two servants, called Sara and Alice, who did her
shopping and ran errands. They fulfilled rather the same role
as extern sisters in contemplative convents today. These
women do not feel called to the seclusion of their sisters inside
the enclosure, who never leave their convent, but feel called to
serve them and act as essential intermediaries between the
cloistered nuns and the world. The life of the anchoress was
hard, but she did not necessarily give herself over to excessive
penance. We have seen that all our mystics stress the importance of attending to the needs of the body. All argue that the
contemplative life is quite hard enough without seeking an
extravagant asceticism that could weaken the body and keep
the contemplative from prayer.

We do not know exactly when Julian was immured. It
has been suggested that she had once been a Benedictine nun
of the convent of Carrow, which was situated near the church

where she eventually had her cell: to this day Benedictine
nuns take the title "Dame," the honorary title of any woman
of rank at this time. But there is no evidence that Julian had
ever been a nun before her immurement, nor is there anything distinctively Benedictine about her spirituality. She
may well have lived in her parents' house before her enclosure: when she describes the circumstances of her visions in
Revelations of Divine Love, she says that there were a large
number of people around her bed and that priests were able
to come and go as they pleased, which would not always
have been possible in an anchorage. But we cannot be certain: all we know about Julian is what she tells us herself in
her book.

In *Revelations of Divine Love,* Julian describes the climactic
experience of her life, which took place in about 1372 when
she was thirty years old. She was extremely ill at the time. We
do not know anything about the nature of her illness. Was it
purely physical or did it have a psychosomatic dimension, as
her sudden and dramatic recovery could indicate? Naturally
nobody would have made this distinction at the time, and
certainly Julian and all her friends thought that she was at
death's door. When a priest came to give her the Last Rites,
she gazed on the crucifix that he held before her eyes and felt
her illness leave her. She fell into a trance and for about five
hours received fifteen consecutive visions and revelations in
which she saw Christ, the Virgin Mary, and the Trinity itself
and heard Jesus' explanations of these "showings." In the
morning, Julian came to herself and, to her dismay, she felt
her illness returning. For a while she thought that her visions
had been a delirium, but then fell into an exhausted sleep
when she received her sixteenth revelation in a dream that
reassured her and made her deeply ashamed of her doubts.
Julian then made a full recovery and lived for another forty
years. She never had any more visions, but spent the rest of

her life pondering the meaning of her sixteen revelations of God's love.

Other people, in widely different cultures and circumstances, have had a very similar experience. Thus, like Julian, the Prophet Muhammad said that his revelations seemed to come to him in two ways: some were clear and others were obscure and very difficult to understand. St. Teresa of Ávila also spoke of the obscure type of revelation, which both Julian and Muhammad described as "spiritual visions":

> *One sees nothing, either within or without, but while seeing nothing the soul understands quite clearly who it is and where it is and sometimes even what he means to tell it. How and by what means it understands it does not know, but so it is, and while this is happening it cannot fail to know it.*[1]

This type of religious experience is often traumatic. Where mystics like the author of *The Cloud of Unknowing* and Walter Hilton insist that their apprehension of the divine brings with it a calm joy that has nothing to do with either physical or emotional sensation, these prophetic visionaries feel like Julian, that the shock of the divine impact has brought them close to death. When Isaiah had his vision of God in the Temple, he cried aloud in anguish that he was lost: even the angels could not bear the sight of the divine majesty. They shielded themselves from it with their wings, but Isaiah had gazed upon the Lord of Hosts with his own impure eyes. Jeremiah experienced God as a pain that invaded his every limb, and Muhammad said that he never received a revelation without feeling that his soul was being torn from his body.

Unlike the mystic, the prophetic visionary believes that he undergoes this fearful experience for the sake of mankind: God does not send these revelations for their own edification but for the sake of their people. Often these prophets saw themselves as reformers, who had a vocation to transform the religious vision of their time. The prophets of Israel reformed the old tribal religion of the Hebrews, brought them a more transcendent conception of God and a deeper morality. Muhammad believed that he had to reform the old pagan religion of al-Llah, the High God of the Arabs. Teresa of Ávila became one of the great reformers of the sixteenth century. True, she did not reform dogma or the social organization of the church like Luther or Calvin. She reformed the religious life of her time for both men and women, teaching them to distinguish between a good and an unhealthy spirituality. These reformers, however, were not passive recipients of a message from on high. They were engaged in a creative and demanding attempt to revise the religion of their day and transform it from within. In his classic book *The Prophets*, Abraham Heschel has shown that Amos, Hosea, Jeremiah, and Isaiah all considered their own input to be a crucial part of their message. Similarly, Julian was not afraid to put her own words and reflections onto the lips of Christ when she wrote her book.

Julian had a humbler conception of her task than the other prophetic reformers I have mentioned, who all experienced God as an absolute imperative to action and felt that they had a mission to defy the religious and secular establishment of their day. Julian did not feel called to reform the church or to take part in public life: she remained a loyal daughter of Mother Church and stayed in seclusion for the rest of her life. But she did believe that her revelations had not been bestowed upon her for herself but for everybody. Her book asked Christians to take a deeper look at some of their religious beliefs. How, she asks, can we account for evil in a world that has been created by a good God? How can a God, in whom there is no evil, love sinful creatures like ourselves? The problem of evil had exercised people in all three traditions of historical monotheism and nobody has ever been able to find a logical way of reconciling it with the concept of the one God. Julian's solution does not make rational sense, but it does reverberate emotionally with an important dimension of the Christian religion of love, which sometimes gets lost in the more cerebral doctrinal formulations of the faith. The problem of sin would be a key theme in the sixteenth-century reformations. This was an age of high anxiety in the West, when people felt deeply disturbed by the vision of God's purity and their own failings. Like Julian, who tells us that she wrestled for years with the problem of sin, Luther and St. Teresa both struggled for some twenty years with a paralyzing sense of their own sinfulness. Like Julian, perhaps, Teresa also had an illness that may well have had a psychological aspect and that brought her to the brink of death; her autobiography and spiritual writings show how she brought herself a physical and spiritual healing. Calvin and his successors came up with the dark doctrine of predestination to explain the fearful paradox of God's love and his implacable wrath. Julian reached a far smaller audience than any of these later reformers and she has never had a decisive effect on the history of Christianity as they did, but she has acquired a considerable following in our own day.

It is not difficult to see why Julian has become so popular in the twentieth century and has inspired writers as different as T. S. Eliot and Iris Murdoch. In recent years people have found the doctrines of Christianity increasingly difficult, but a visionary like Julian penetrates the cerebral crust of the religious experience, which has little to do with logic and reason, to reach its core. In doing so, she touches on themes that are common to the mystical traditions of other faiths. Her vision of God in the depths of the self is reminiscent of the basic insights of Buddhists, Hindus and Sufis. Like Jewish and Muslim mystics, Julian stresses the paradox of God's mysterious need for mankind and also explores the notion of the female dimension of God, a frequent theme in Kabbalism and Sufism.

A religious insight like Julian's shows that a passive unquestioning acceptance of received dogma is not enough. Each age and each individual has to make the imaginative effort to appropriate the religious tradition and make it their own, as Julian did. She does not expect her readers to accept her own conclusions verbatim, but urges them to make a similar creative attempt to listen for the deeper implications of the Christian message, to reach through the dogmas and intellectual propositions, which can never do justice to the ineffable mystery of the divine, and touch the heart of the faith. In the West, where many people have lost the will to create a faith for themselves and where many have fallen into despair, Julian's imaginative approach to religion shows a possible way forward.

Revelations of Divine Love

Chapter 2: Julian Asks God for Three Gifts

These revelations were shown to a simple uneducated creature in the year of our Lord 1373 on 13 May. Previously this creature had asked God for three gifts. The first was a sympathetic knowledge of his Passion; the second was to suffer from a physical illness when she was still a young woman of thirty; and the third was to receive three wounds from God.[2]

As to the first gift, I seemed to have some feeling for Christ's Passion but I wanted still more, by God's grace. I wished that I had actually been present at the time with Mary Magdalene and Christ's other friends, and I wanted to see the physical agony of my Savior for myself so that I could understand it better. I also wanted to feel sympathy with our Lady and all his true friends who witnessed his suffering. That was the only vision of God that I wanted in this life, and the reason for my request was to have a more accurate understanding of Christ's Passion after the revelation.

The second gift was due to my sorrow for my sins. I really wanted to have a serious illness that would bring me to the point of death so that I would receive the Last Rites of Holy Church in the sincere belief that I was going to die and that all the other creatures who saw me should think the same. There was nothing to comfort me in this earthly life. During this illness, I wanted to suffer all the physical and spiritual agony that I would have if I really were going to die and to have all the terror and confusion that the devils would inflict upon me — everything, in fact, short of actually passing away. The idea was that this would purify me, by God's mercy, so that in future, because of that illness, I would be more devoted to God and I might even die more quickly because I wanted to be with God soon.

There was one condition: when I requested these two things, I said, "Lord, you know what I want. If it is your will that I have it . . . and if it is not your will, good Lord, don't be angry, because the only thing I want is that your will be done."

My third request was that, by God's grace and the teaching of Holy Church, I conceived a great desire to receive three wounds during my lifetime, namely, the wound of true contrition, the wound of genuine compassion, and the wound of a serious longing for God. I made no conditions when I asked for this.

I forgot my first two requests, but the third was constantly in my mind.

Chapter 3: She Becomes Ill

So, when I was thirty years and six months old, God sent me a physical illness that prostrated me for three days and three nights. On the fourth night I received all the rites of Holy Church and didn't expect to live till morning. But I lingered for another two days, and during the third night I thought that I was on the point of death and everybody who was with me thought the same.

And, as I was still young, I thought it was a great shame that I was going to die, not because I had anything in the world to live for or because I was afraid of the pain — because I put my trust in God's mercy — but I wanted to live so that I could have the chance to love God better and could, therefore, know and love him more perfectly in the bliss of heaven. My life had been so paltry and short compared with that eternal happiness that it seemed nothing at all. So I thought: "Good Lord, let the end of my life be to your glory!" My reason and my suffering both assured me that I was going to die, and I surrendered wholeheartedly to God's will.

I endured till daybreak in this state, and by then my body was dead from the waist down. I felt that I wanted to be helped and supported to sit up so that my heart could wait more easily on God's will and I could keep my mind on God while I was still alive.

My priest had been summoned to be present at the end, and when he arrived, my eyes were fixed and I could not speak. He held his crucifix before my face and said, "I have brought you the image of your Creator and Redeemer. Look upon it and take comfort!"

I thought that I was all right as I was because my eyes were fixed on heaven, whither I believed that, with God's mercy, I was about to go. But I agreed, all the same, to gaze upon the crucifix instead, if I could. And so I did. It seemed to me that I might be able to look straight ahead longer than I could gaze upward.

Then my sight began to fail and the room became as dark as night around me, except for the crucifix, which seemed to be lit up — I didn't know how. Everything but the crucifix seemed terrifying, as if the room had been invaded by demons.

Then the upper part of my body began to die and I had scarcely any sensation left and had trouble breathing. I was certain that I was at death's door.

But at that moment, my pain suddenly vanished and I was as well — especially in the upper part of my body — as I had ever been in my life!

I was astonished by this dramatic change because it seemed to be a special miracle of God and not a natural cure. But despite feeling so comfortable, I still did not believe that I was going to live, and I wasn't entirely happy about this sudden change, but I thought I would much rather leave the world behind.

Then it suddenly occurred to me that I should ask for the second wound of our Lord's gracious gift: that my body might perfectly experience and understand his blessed Passion. I wanted his pains to be my pains. I wanted to suffer with him and so conceive a longing for God. I didn't want a physical vision or revelation from God but a compassion that I would naturally feel for our Lord Jesus, who became a mortal man for love of us. And that is why I wanted to suffer with him.

Chapter 4: The First Revelation

At that moment I suddenly saw red blood trickling down from beneath the crown of thorns on the crucifix. It was as hot, fresh, and plentiful as it had been at the time of the Passion, when this garland had been pressed onto the head of him who was both God and man and who had endured all this for me. I was utterly convinced that it was God and no one else who showed me this.

At the same time, the Trinity filled my heart to the brim with joy and I realized what heaven was like for those who reached it. For the Trinity is God: God is the Trinity; the Trinity is our Creator and Preserver; the Trinity is our everlasting love, joy and happiness, through our Lord Jesus Christ. I was shown this in the first revelation for, as I see it, whenever Jesus is mentioned, the whole of the blessed Trinity should be understood.

And I said, "Blessed be God!" I said it very loudly and with great reverence. I was overcome with astonishment and wonder that he, who is so holy and awesome, should be so friendly to a sinful creature who was still living in her wretched body.

I thought that this revelation had been sent to prepare me for a temptation, for I expected God to allow me to be tempted by demons before I died. Because of the vision of the blessed Passion and the experience of the Godhead, I was confident that I had enough strength for myself — and, indeed, for everybody else! — to withstand the fiends of hell and any temptation of the spirit.

And then he brought our blessed Lady into my mind. I saw her in a spiritual manner as though she were actually present in body: a simple, humble young girl, little more than a child, at the age she was when she conceived. And God gave me a glimpse of the wisdom and beauty of her soul and I realized her deep reverence for God, her Creator, and her great wonder that he wanted to be born of a creature he had made. It was this wisdom and honesty — her understanding of the greatness of her Creator and her own littleness — that made her reply so humbly to Gabriel: "Behold the handmaid of the Lord." In this vision, I realized that she was more valuable and had received more grace than any other creature except for the humanity of Christ.

Chapter 5: "It Is All That Is Made"

At the same time, our Lord showed me, in a spiritual manner, how intimately he loves us. I saw that he is everything that is good and which supports us. He clothes us in his love, envelops us and embraces us. He laps us round in his tender love and he will never abandon us. As I understand it, he is everything that is good.

He also showed me a tiny thing in the palm of my hand, the size of a hazelnut. I looked at this with the eye of my soul and thought, "What is this?" And this is the answer that came to me, *It is all that is made.* I was astonished that it managed to survive: it was so small that I thought that it might disintegrate. And in my mind I heard this answer: "It lives on and will live on forever because God loves it." So every single thing owes its existence to the love of God.

I saw that this tiny thing had three properties that were essential to it. The first is that God made it; the second is that God loves it; the third, that God preserves it. But I cannot say what this Creator, Preserver, and Lover is. Until I am united to him in my essential being, there will be no true happiness for me — by that I mean that until I am linked to him so closely that there is absolutely nothing between God and me. We need to know how tiny creation is and to reckon all creatures as nothing if we are to love the God who is uncreated. This is the reason why we are never entirely at peace in heart and soul: we seek rest in such tiny things that cannot give us rest, and we do not realize that our God is All-Mighty, All-Wise, and All-Good. For he is true rest. God wants to be known and it pleases him when we rest in him, for nothing less than him will satisfy us. That is why no soul finds rest until it has discounted all things. When it has deliberately detached itself for the love of him who is in all things, then the soul will find rest of spirit.

Our Lord God also showed me what pleasure it gives him when a vulnerable soul comes to him, simply, openly, and as a friend. For when I think over this revelation, it seems to me that when the Holy Ghost touches the soul, it longs for God in this way: "O God, of your goodness, give yourself to me: for you are enough for me and, if I want to be worthy of you, I cannot really ask for anything less. If I do ask for anything less, I shall remain in need. Only in you do I have everything."

The soul responds to such words lovingly and they come very close to the will of God and his goodness. For his goodness takes in every single one of his creatures and all his blessed works and it surpasses them eternally. For he is eternity itself and has made us for himself alone. He has redeemed us by his blessed Passion and preserves us in his blessed love. And he does all this because he is goodness itself.

From Chapter 8: Lady Julian's Visions Are Not for Herself but for Everybody

Our Lord showed me all this in the first revelation in a leisurely and unhurried manner. My physical sight had failed, but I continued to see and understand with the eye of my mind and I watched with reverence and awe, rejoicing in everything I saw. And I was bold enough to want to see more, if that was his will, or else to keep the present vision for a longer time.

Throughout this whole experience, I was inspired with a great love for my fellow Christians and I wanted them to be able to see and know what I saw. I knew that it would be a comfort to them. This vision was for everybody. Then I said to the people around me: "This is the Day of Judgment for me." I said this because I thought I was going to die. (As I understand it, a man is judged on the day of his death and his eternal fate is decided forever.) I said this because I wanted them to love God better and to remind them, by my own example, how short life is. I was still expecting to die, and this was a source of wonder as well as a little worrying, because I thought that the vision was intended for those who had to go on living. So even when I seem to be talking about myself, I am really talking about all my fellow Christians, for the spiritual meaning of the revelation taught me that this was what God intended. So I beg you all, for God's sake, and advise you for your own good to stop thinking about the poor creature who had the revelation. Look at God instead, with all your might and with intelligence and humility, so that he will be willing to show it to everybody in his considerate love and endless goodness, to the great comfort of us all. For God wants you to receive it with great joy and pleasure, as if Jesus had revealed it to you all.

Chapter 9: Julian Is No Better Than Anybody Else

I am not a good person simply because I have had this revelation but only if I love God more perfectly. You are better than me if you love God more. I am not speaking to clever people, who know all this already, but to simple folk for their comfort and consolation. We all need comfort. I certainly didn't receive a revelation because God loved me better than other humble souls in a state of grace, for I am quite sure that there are plenty of people who love God more than I do who have never had a revelation or a vision and rely only on the ordinary teaching of Holy Church. When I look at myself in particular, I see that I am nothing at all but I hope that I am united in charity with all my fellow Christians.

All men who are going to be saved must rely upon this communion of Christians. For, in my view, God is everything that is good and he has made the whole of creation and he loves what he has made. Anybody who loves his fellow Christians for God's sake, loves everything that exists. For everything is included in that portion of humanity who are going to be saved — by that I mean the whole of creation and the Maker of everything too! For God is in man and God is in everything. And I hope, by God's grace, that anyone who looks at it like this will be instructed correctly and get whatever consolation he needs.

I am only talking about the people who are going to be saved, for that was all that God revealed to me. I believe what Holy Church believes, preaches, and teaches. For the faith of Holy Church, as I had always understood it, and which, by God's grace, I hope had always guided my conduct and beliefs, was always before my eyes. I neither wanted nor intended to receive any revelation that was contrary to this, and it was with this intention that I contemplated this revelation so carefully. Throughout this blessed revelation, everything I saw agreed with God's official teaching.

The revelations came to me in three ways: with the eyes of my body, by a word that was imaginatively conceived in my mind, and by a spiritual vision. I cannot describe the spiritual vision as clearly and fully as I would like, but I trust that God almighty will enable you to understand it in a spiritual way and more sweetly than I am able to describe, with his great goodness and love.

From Chapter 11: How Can Anything Be Amiss?

After this I saw God, as it were, concentrated in a Point (I mean that I "saw" it in my mind). In this vision I understood that he is in all things. I gazed at it and meditated, and my seeing and thinking were tinged with fear. I was thinking: "What is sin?"

For I realized that in fact God does everything, however small it is. And indeed I saw that nothing happens by chance or luck but everything is caused by the providence and wisdom of God. If things seem to happen by chance or luck, that is because of our blindness and lack of foresight. Things that God's wise providence foresaw from before the beginning of time and that he so justly and honorably always brings in due course to their proper end, drop on us suddenly and we don't understand what is happening. That is why, in our blindness and lack of foresight, we say: these are accidents and strokes of luck. But they are not like that to our Lord God.

So I have to agree that anything that happens is done well because our Lord God does it. I did not at this time see how creatures act but how God works in his creatures, because he is the end of all things and he does everything. And I was quite sure that he does no sin!

And from this point I went on to see that sin is not an action, for no sin was revealed to me in all this activity. I did not want to speculate about this, but instead I turned toward our Lord and looked at what he wanted to show me. And thus, the righteousness of God's actions was shown to my soul, as far as it was possible at that time. Righteousness has two good characteristics: it is correct and it is complete, and so are all God's works. It does not need mercy or grace because they are righteous too. There is nothing missing.

On another occasion when God gave me a revelation, I saw sin as it really is. I will describe this later as well as how God employs his mercy and grace.

This revelation made me understand that our Lord wants the soul to turn wholly to him and gaze at him and generally on all his works. For they are entirely good. His actions are consoling and sweet and bring great comfort to the soul who rejects a human and blind way of judging things in favor of the beautiful and delightful judgment of God. A man regards some things as well done and others as evil, but our Lord does not regard them like that. For as all natural things have really been performed by God, so everything that has been done has somehow been done by God. For it is easy to understand that the best deed has been performed well and as the best and the highest deed has been done, so the least deed has been done just as well. All this is due to the plan that God ordained from all eternity. He is the only one who acts.

I saw with complete certainty that God never changes his purpose in anything and that he never will. Everything has been known to him from the start, according to his plan. Before anything was created, everything was set in its proper place, as it was to remain forever. Nothing was to fail of its purpose. He made everything in his overflowing benevolence, and thus the Trinity is forever entirely satisfied with everything he has done.

And he revealed all this to me and filled me with happiness. It was as though he were saying: *Look! I am God! Look! I am in all things. Look! I do everything! I hold my work always in my hands and I will never let them fall. Look! I am guiding everything to the end I ordained for it from before the beginning of time, with the same power, wisdom and love with which I created it! So how can anything be amiss?*

From Chapter 22: The Sufferings of Christ

Then our good Lord Jesus Christ said, *Are you entirely happy that I have suffered for you?* "Yes, good Lord, thank you," I said. "Yes, good Lord, bless you." Then Jesus, our kind Lord, said, *If you are glad, I am glad too: it is a joy, a happiness, and an eternal satisfaction to me ever to have suffered my passion for you. And if I could possibly suffer more, I would suffer more.*

With these words: *If I could possibly suffer more, I would suffer more,* I saw that if he could, he would have suffered over and over again and that his love would not have let him rest until he had done it. I gazed very carefully to find out how often he would have died if he could, but the number was incalculable and my reason could make no sense of it. And yet however many times he died, he would count it as nothing compared with his love for us.

For though the sweet humanity of Christ could only suffer once, his goodness would make him ready to do this continuously, every day if necessary. For if he said that he would create a new heaven and a new earth out of love for me, that would be a small matter in comparison. If he wanted to, he could do it every day without any trouble at all. But to be willing to die for love of me an incalculable number of times, that is the supreme gesture that our Lord could make to the soul of man, as I see it. This is what he meant: *How should I not, out of love for you, do all I can for you? It would not grieve me, since because of my love for you, I would like to die often and would take no notice of the agonizing pain.*

And here I saw . . . that the love that caused him to suffer surpasses all his pain as heaven towers over the earth. For his pain was a noble and worthy deed, an act of love that performed in time. But his love itself had no beginning, is and ever shall be. Because of this love he said these sweet words: *If I could suffer more, I would suffer more.* He did not say, *If I had to suffer more,* for even if it were unnecessary, if it was possible for him to suffer more he would do it.

Chapter 24: "See How I Have Loved Thee!"

Then, with a cheerful expression, our Lord regarded his side and rejoiced as he gazed at it. While he looked he drew me with my meager understanding by way of the same wound in his side. There he showed me a fair and pleasant place, which was big enough for all humanity to rest in peace and love. With that, he reminded me of that most precious blood and water that he allowed to pour from him for love. And, gazing still, he showed me his blessed heart, which was broken into two pieces.

With his sweet pleasure, he helped me to understand at least a little how the blessed Godhead was inspiring a poor soul to perceive and, as it were, to meditate upon the endless love of God that has no beginning, exists now, and will last forever. At the same time, our good Lord said joyously, *See how I have loved you!* as though he were saying, *Look, my darling, at your Lord, your God, your Creator and your endless joy, see what satisfaction and happiness I find in your salvation. If you love me, rejoice with me.*

And again, this blessed word was spoken to help me to understand: *See how I have loved you! Look and see that I loved you so much before I died for your sake that I wanted to die for you. And now I have died for you and willingly suffered all that I could. Now all my bitter agony and all my painful work has been transformed into endless you, for you and for me. How can you pray for anything that pleases me and I not gladly grant it? I take delight in your holiness and the eternal joy and happiness you will share with me.*

I have expressed my understanding of the words *See how I have loved you!* as simply as I can. Our good Lord revealed this to make us happy and peaceful.

Chapter 26: God Is the Essence of All Things

Then our Lord seemed to reveal himself in a greater splendor than ever before. This taught me that our soul will never know rest until it comes to him and knows that he is complete joy, friendly and courteous, joyful and life itself.

Our Lord Jesus frequently said: *It is I; it is I; it is I who am sublime; it is I whom you love; it is I whom you enjoy; it is I whom you serve; it is I whom you long for; it is I whom you desire; it is I whom you think about; it is I who am all things. It is I whom Holy Church preaches and teaches; it is I who revealed myself to you here.*

He said so many things that my feeble mind could not take them all in or understand them. In my opinion, there are no more excellent words than these. They comprise . . . oh, I cannot explain! All I can say is that the joy I saw in this particular revelation exceeds all that the heart can wish for and a soul desire. So I have not recorded all his words here. But let each person receive them as our Lord intended, according to the grace that God gives him to understand and to love.

From Chapter 27: Sin Is Necessary

After this our Lord brought my mind back to the longing I had previously had for him. And I saw that only sin held me back. And, taking a wider view, I looked on the situation of us all and thought: "If only there had been no sin, we should all have been spotless and like our Lord, as he created us."

And so in the old days, I had been stupid enough to wonder why the powerful, foreseeing wisdom of God had not prevented sin from the start; for then, I thought, everything would have been all right. I really shouldn't have indulged this line of thought, as it made me depressed and sorrowful, without any reason or justification. But Jesus, who informed me in this vision of everything that I needed to know, gave me this answer: *It was necessary that there should be sin, but all will be well, all will be well, every conceivable thing will be well.*

In this simple word "sin," our Lord reminded me in a general way of all the things that are not good, and of the shame, contempt, and utter humiliation he suffered for us in his life and death. And of the pain and suffering of all the creatures he has made, physical and spiritual. For we have all experienced something of this annihilation and if we follow Jesus, our Master, we must be totally annihilated until we are purified in our mortal flesh and in the depths of our being. I saw all this and I saw too all the suffering that has ever been or ever can be and I understood that no pain was greater than the supreme suffering of Christ. This was all revealed in a flash and quickly turned into consolation, because our Lord would never want the soul to be frightened by this fearful sight.

But I did not see *sin*, because I believe that it has no substance and no real existence. It can only be known by the pain which it causes. This pain does exist, in my view, but only for a limited time. It purifies us, gives us self-knowledge, and makes us beg for mercy. The passion of our Lord is comforting to us and an antidote to this — for this is his blessed will. It is because of this tender love for everybody who is going to be saved that our Lord immediately consoles us so sweetly, as though he said, *It is true that sin is the cause of all this pain, but all will be well, all will be well and every conceivable thing will be well.*

These words were spoken very tenderly with no hint of blame, either to me or to any of those who are saved. So it would be most perverse of me to blame or question God because of my sin, since he doesn't blame me for it. In these words I saw a marvelous and sublime mystery, which is hidden in God and which he will fully disclose to us in heaven. When we know this we shall indeed see the reason why he allowed sin to exist. In this vision, we shall endlessly rejoice in our Lord God.

From Chapter 31: The Vulnerability of God

And thus our good Lord answered all my questions and doubts and to comfort me said, *I have the power to make every-*

thing right; I can make everything right; I intend to make everything right and I will do it. You will see for yourself that all will be well.

When he says, *I have the power,* I understand that this refers to the Father; when he says, *I can,* I take it to mean the Son, and when he says, *I intend to,* I understand this to be the Holy Spirit. When he says, *I will,* this means the unity of the Trinity: three Persons and one Truth. When he says, *You will see for yourself,* I understand this to mean the unity of the whole of redeemed humanity with the Trinity. In these five utterances, God intends us to be wholly enveloped in rest and peace.

For since Christ is our head, he is glorified and incapable of pain. But since he is also the Body in which all his members are united, he is not yet fully glorified and impassible. Therefore, the same desire and thirst that our Lord had on the Cross — and I believe that this desire, longing, and thirst was with him from before the beginning of time — he still has and will continue to have until the moment when the last soul to be saved reaches heaven.

For just as there is in God a quality of sympathy and pity, so too there is also the quality of thirst and longing. And by the power of this longing in Christ, we are made to long for him in our turn. Without such a longing, no soul will reach heaven. The attribute of thirst and longing derives, like his pity, from God's eternal goodness. And though, in my view, longing and pity are two different things, this spiritual thirst of God is rooted in his goodness: this thirst is a desire in God that draws us up to his own bliss as long as we need it. And all this was revealed in this vision of his compassion; it will come to an end on the Day of Judgment.

Thus he has pity and compassion for us and he longs to possess us. But his wisdom and love will not allow the end to come until the right moment.

Chapter 32: The Problem of Evil

On one occasion, our Lord God said, *All will be well,* and on another he said, *You will see that every conceivable thing will be well.* The soul can find several meanings in these two utterances.

One was that he wants us to know that he not only looks after the important, grand things, but also little and small, humble and simple things. That is what he meant when he said, *Every conceivable thing will be well,* because he wants us to know that not even the smallest thing will be forgotten.

Another meaning is this: we see that evil things happen and they cause such harm that we cannot imagine that any good will come of them. As we contemplate these things in grief and sorrow, we cannot resign ourselves as we should to the positive contemplation of God. The reason for this is that our intellect is now so blind, so debased, and so simple that we are incapable of knowing the marvelous and sublime Power, Wisdom, and Goodness of the blessed Trinity. This is what he meant when he said, *You will see for yourself that every conceivable thing will be well.* It is as if he said, *Take care to have faith and trust now and in the end you will really see the whole thing with perfect joy.*

And similarly, in those same words quoted earlier, *I have the power to make all things well,* I see a great comfort in the work that God still has to do. There is a deed that the blessed Trinity shall perform on the Last Day, I think, but when this deed will be performed and how it will be done is not known to any of God's creatures under Christ and will remain hidden until it happens.

The reason why God wants us to know about this future deed is that he wants us to be more at peace and more easy in our minds and to stop thinking about disturbing things that inhibit our true joy in him. This great deed of our

Lord God, planned before the beginning of time, treasured and hidden in his bosom, is known only to himself: by it he will make all things well. For just as the blessed Trinity created everything from nothing, so too the Trinity will make all those things well which are not right.

I found this a marvelous insight, and as I considered our faith I marveled, saying, "Our faith is grounded in God's word and our faith tells us that we who believe in God's words will be entirely saved. One article of our faith is that many creatures will be damned: for example, the angels, whose pride caused them to fall from heaven, who are now demons; and many here on earth who died outside the faith of Holy Church — that is, the pagans and those who received baptism, but who live un-Christian lives and die out of charity. All these will be condemned to hell forever, as Holy Church teaches and commands us to believe." When I thought about all this, it seemed impossible to me that everything would be well, as our Lord was now revealing to me.

I had no other answer during this revelation about our Lord God, but only this: *What is impossible to you is not impossible to me. I shall keep my word in all things and I shall make all things well.* So, by the grace of God, I was taught that I must hold firmly to the faith, as I had previously understood it, and at the same time that I should firmly believe that all things will be well, as our Lord God had revealed to me.

For the great deed that our Lord is going to perform will enable him to keep his word and will make all that is not well right. How that will be done nobody under Christ knows — and never will know until it has been performed. That is how I understood our Lord's meaning at the time.

From Chapter 41: God Is the Foundation of Our Prayer

Then our Lord revealed this about prayer, which, I believe, has two qualities: righteousness and trust. But often our trust is not perfect, because we are not sure that God listens to us. We think this is because we are so unworthy and because we don't feel anything, for often we are as dry and barren after prayer as we were before. This perception of our dullness is the cause of our weakness. For this is how I have experienced it myself.

Our Lord introduced this idea into my mind immediately, when he revealed these words: *I am the ground in which your prayer is rooted. First I want you to pray and next I make you want it. After that I enable you to pray and so you do pray. How, then, can you possibly not have what you ask for?* . . .

Our Lord is made happy and cheerful when we pray. He waits for it and wants it because, by his grace, he makes us like himself in our human nature. This is his blessed will. So he says, *Pray inwardly, even if you don't enjoy it; it helps you even if you don't feel it or see it. For when you are dry and barren, sick and weak, your prayer is especially pleasing to me, even though you don't enjoy it very much. That is true of all prayer made in faith.*

Because he wants to give us a reverent and endless gratitude, he is eager to see us pray continuously. God accepts the goodwill and effort his servant makes, no matter what we are feeling like. He is pleased that we struggle with our prayers and our lives, with the help of grace, and that we consciously direct all our powers to him until we possess him whom we seek in complete joy.

From Chapter 42: Our Prayer Is a Gift from God

There are some particular things that God wants us to understand about prayer. The first is that we should know through whom and how our prayer begins. He showed us "through whom" when he said, *I am the ground,* and he showed us "how" when he said, *It is my will.*

The second thing he wants us to know is the best way to use our prayer. In fact, it means that our will should be joyfully directed to our Lord's will. That is what he means when he says, *I make you want it.* The third thing is that we should know the fruit and purpose of our prayer; that is, we should be united with our Lord and become like him in all things. This was his intention and purpose in that lovely lesson. He will help us and we will make his word God. Blessed be he!

This is what our Lord wants: that we should be magnanimous in our prayer and our trust. If we do not trust as much as we pray, we are not really giving honor to God in our prayer. We also torment ourselves and do ourselves harm. I think that the reason is that we have not fully realized that our Lord is the ground from which our prayer grows, nor do we realize that our prayer is itself a gift of his love. If we knew this, it would make us believe that we will have everything we want as a gift from our Lord. I am certain that nobody asks for mercy and grace in good earnest unless grace and mercy had already been given to him.

Sometimes it seems to us that we have prayed for a long time and have not been answered. We should not be depressed about this. I am sure that our Lord's intention is that we either wait for a better time or for more grace and a better gift. He wants us to have a deep knowledge of the fact that God himself is the essence of everything. He wants us to root our understanding in this knowledge as strongly, deliberately, pray; wondering, enjoying, venerating, fearing him with such sweetness and delight that for the duration we can only pray in the way he inspires us. As I know very well, the more the soul sees of God, the more it longs for him, by his grace.

But when we don't see him like this, we feel the need to pray to Jesus all the more, because of our failure and helplessness. When the soul is tossed about, distressed and abandoned in its restlessness, then it is time to pray so that it may become pliable and yielding to God. But, of course, the soul can by no means make God flexible to itself, because he is constant in his love.

And this is what I saw: when we realize our need for prayer, then our good Lord follows us, encouraging our desire. And when he gives us the special grace to see him clearly, we need nothing else and we follow him and he draws us to himself in love. For I realized that his wondrous and abundant goodness is the fulfillment of all our abilities. I also saw that his continuous work in every single thing is done so kindly, so wisely, and so powerfully that we cannot imagine or think about it. We can do nothing but gaze at him with joy and a sublime and strong desire to be totally united to him, to live in him, to rejoice in his love and delight in his goodness.

Chapter 44: Humankind and the Trinity

During these revelations, God often showed me that man was always doing God's will and honoring him. In the first revelation, he showed *what* this work actually was in the marvelous example of our blessed Lady, St. Mary, and the way truth and wisdom were at work in her soul. I hope, with the grace of the Holy Spirit, to show *how* I saw that it was done.

Truth sees God and wisdom contemplates God and

and sincerely as we can. He wants us to plant ourselves i
firmly and permanently and live in this fact.

From Chapter 43: Prayer Unites Us to God

Prayer unites the soul to God. Once the soul has been
restored to itself by means of grace it is like God in its essential
and deepest nature, but in fact it is often unlike God because
of the sins that men commit. It is then that prayer makes it
clear that the soul must adopt God's will. It strengthens the
conscience and enables a man to receive more grace. God
teaches us to pray like this and to cultivate a great trust that
we shall get what we ask for. For he looks upon us with love
and wants us to participate in his good work and that is why
he inspires us to pray for what he wants to give us! He gives
us an eternal reward for this prayer and goodwill, even
though the prayer is a gift in itself.

This was revealed in these words: *and so you do pray.* In
this utterance, God shows as much pleasure and satisfaction
as if he were beholden to us for all our good works. Yet it is he
who does them all! Because we beg him to do what he sees to
be good, it is as if he said, *What can please me more than that you
pray to me ardently, wisely, and earnestly to do the thing that I was
going to do anyway?*

This is the way that a soul conforms itself to God in
prayer.

But when our courteous Lord gives us the grace of
revealing himself to our soul, we have what we desire. At that
time we are not interested in praying for anything else, be
cause all our attention and intent is fixed on contemplatir
him. This is a very exalted type of prayer that cannot, in r
opinion, be described, because the origin of our prayer !
been united to the sight and vision of the One to whom

from these two springs the third: a holy, wondering pleasure in God, which is love. Indeed, wherever truth and wisdom are, love is there too, proceeding from them both. This is all God's doing, for he is eternal, sovereign Truth, eternal, sovereign Wisdom, eternal, sovereign Love, and he is uncreated. Man's soul has been created by God and has the same qualities, only they are created. It always does what it was created to do: it sees God, it contemplates him, and it loves him. So God takes delight in his creature and the creature in God in an eternal act of wonder.

In this wonder, he sees his God, his Lord, his Creator, so exalted, immense, and good that the creature seems nothing in comparison. But the brightness and splendor of Truth and Wisdom make him see and bear witness to the fact that he is created for Love and in that Love God eternally preserves him.

From Chapter 49: God Is Never Angry

It was astonishing to me and I considered it carefully in later years that during these revelations I was continually shown that our Lord God, as far as he himself is concerned, does not have to forgive because he is unable to be angry. It would be impossible for him! This was the revelation: that the whole of life is grounded and rooted in love and that without love we cannot live. So a soul that is given the special grace of gazing deeply into the sublime and marvelous goodness of God and sees that we are eternally united to him in love, finds that it is quite impossible for God to be angry. Anger and friendship are mutually exclusive. And he that weakens and destroys our anger and makes us humble and gentle, must himself surely need to be loving, humble, and gentle and that is the direct opposite of anger.

I saw with absolute certainty that, where our Lord is, peace is the rule and there is no place for anger. I saw no anger of any kind in God, no matter how long I looked. Indeed, as I see it, if God were able to be angry for one second, we should have no life, abode, or existence! For just as we derive our existence from the endless Power of God, his endless Wisdom and endless Goodness, so are we preserved by the same qualities. Though we poor wretches experience conflict and strife within ourselves, we are still wholly enveloped in God's humility, goodness, and kindness. For I saw very clearly that our eternal friendship, our abode, our life, and our existence is in God.

The same eternal goodness that preserves us, even when we sin, and prevents us from perishing, keeps trying to make peace of our anger and perverse failures. It makes us realize our own need with a true fear and gives us a strong desire to seek forgiveness and ask God to save us. Even though we are at present in misery, distress, and grief, as a result of our blindness and infirmity, our own anger and perversity, we are still kept safe by the mercy of God and we do not perish. But we are not yet in bliss, not yet saved, and are not yet in eternal joy, nor wholly at peace or in love, until we are content with God and his actions and judgments, until we are in love and at peace with ourselves, with our fellow Christians and with all that God loves. That is what love is like and this is what God's goodness does in us.

So I saw that God is our true peace and that he is our true Preserver when we ourselves are not at peace. He continually works to bring us to eternal peace. And so when, by the action of his mercy and grace, we have become humble and gentle, we are really safe. When the soul is really at peace with itself, it is immediately united to God because there can be no anger in God.

From Chapter 53: Nothing Between God and the Soul

I saw that God never began to love mankind. For, just as humanity is bound for eternal bliss in order to satisfy the joy that God prepared for his creation, so mankind has been known and loved from all eternity in the providence of God. For with the eternal assent and agreement of the whole Trinity, the Second Person willed to become the ground and head of this beautiful human nature. We all came from him, we are all comprised in him, and to him we are destined to go in order to find our heaven and everlasting joy. All this was achieved in the providential purpose of the blessed Trinity from before the beginning of time.

For he loved us before he made us, and after we had been created, we loved him. And this is a love that has been created by the essential goodness of the Holy Spirit. This love is powerful by virtue of the Power of the Father, wise by virtue of the Wisdom of the Son. Man's soul is created by God and united to him in the same instant.

And so I understood that man's soul was created from nothing, or rather, it has been made but not out of anything created. Thus, when God created man's body, he took clay from the earth, which is a substance composed of many physical elements. And from all this he made man's body. But he didn't take anything at all when he made man's soul: he just created it. And in this way, created nature was duly united to its Maker, who is essentially uncreated Nature: that is, God. And that is why there neither can nor should be anything at all between God and a man's soul.

Man's soul is preserved whole and entire in God's eternal love, as the revelations show. In this endless love we are guided and preserved by God and will never be lost. For it is his will that we realize that our soul is alive and that this life, through his goodness and grace, will continue in heaven forever, loving, thanking, and praising him. And just as we shall be in eternity, in exactly the same way were we treasured and hidden in God, known and loved by him from before the beginning of time. That is why he wants us to know that the noblest thing he ever created is mankind.

From Chapter 54: "It Was All God!"

How exalted should be our joy that God dwells within our soul! And how much greater should be our joy that our soul dwells with God! Our soul is created to be God's dwelling and the dwelling of the soul is God, who is uncreated. It is a sublime thing to know within ourselves and to see that God, our Creator, lives in our soul. And it is an even greater thing to know and see in an interior manner that our created soul dwells in the substance of God. From that substance of God we are what we are.

And I saw that there was no difference between God and our own substance: but it was, so to speak, all God. Yet my mind realized that our substance was in God, which is to say: God is God and our substance is his creation. For the almighty Truth of the Trinity is our Father, because he created us and preserves us in himself. And the deep Wisdom of the Trinity is our Mother, by whom we are wholly embraced and he by us. The high Goodness of the Trinity is our Lord and we are enveloped by him and he by us. We are enveloped by Father, Son, and Holy Ghost. And Father, Son, and Holy Ghost are enveloped by us: All-Powerfulness, All-Wisdom, and All-Goodness — one God, one Lord.

And our faith is a virtue that springs from our essential nature and enters our soul through the Holy Ghost. Through him all virtues come to us, for there can be no virtue without him. Our faith is simply the correct understanding, correct belief, and sure trust in our essential being: namely, that we are one in God and he is in us, even though we do not see him. This virtue, and all the others that derive from it, achieves great things within us, as God has ordained. For within us is Christ's merciful activity and, through grace, we conform ourselves to him by means of the gifts and virtues of the Holy Ghost. This activity brings it about that we are Christ's children and live Christian lives.

From Chapter 56: The Ground of Our Being

And so I saw with absolute certainty that it is easier for us to arrive at a knowledge of God than to know our own soul. For our soul is so profoundly rooted in God and so endlessly treasured by him that we cannot come to know it unless we have known God first, the Creator to whom we are united. But nevertheless I saw that for our own perfection we must desire to know our own soul, in wisdom and truth. This will teach us to look for it in the right place: that is, in God. And so, by the gracious direction of the Holy Ghost, we know them both together. It doesn't matter whether we are inspired to know God or our own soul; both inspirations are good and true.

God is closer to us than our own soul. For he is the ground in which it is planted and he is the means that keeps our substance and humanity inseparably together. Our soul sits in God, our true rest, and our soul is planted in God, its true strength, and our soul is essentially rooted to God in endless love. And so if we want to know our soul and commune intimately with it, we must look for it in our Lord God, in whom it is enclosed. . . .

Our substance and humanity together can rightly be

called our soul because they are united together in God. That
noble city, the abode of our Lord Jesus Christ, in which he is
enclosed, and our natural substance is enclosed in him just as
his blessed soul is at rest in the Godhead.

And I saw very clearly that we must cultivate longing
and contrition until the time when we are introduced so
deeply into God that we truly know our own soul. And I saw
that it is our good Lord himself who leads us into those
exalted depths with the same love that caused him to create us
and to redeem us in mercy and grace, by virtue of his blessed
passion. But despite all this, we can never reach a perfect
knowledge of God unless we first have a clear knowledge of
our own soul. For until the soul has attained its full potential,
we cannot be entirely holy — that is to say, until our humanity
has been raised to the same level as our Substance, through
the passion of Christ and the merits we have acquired by the
trials that our Lord lays upon us with his mercy and grace.

I had experienced the fleeting touch of God in the soul,
and this was deeply natural. That is to say, our reason is
founded in God, who is the Substance of all natural things.
From this essential nature spring mercy and grace, which
spread over us, causing that activity that fulfills us and makes
our joy complete. They are the ground in which we find our
own increase and fulfillment.

Chapter 58: The Motherhood of the Trinity

God, the Blessed Trinity, is eternal being. Just as he is
eternal and has no beginning, so his intention to make mankind was also eternal. Our beautiful humanity was prepared
first of all in his own Son, the Second Person. And, when he
willed and with the consent of the whole Trinity, he created us
all at the same time. When he created us, he united us to

himself and this union keeps us as pure and noble as when we were first created. It is by means of this precious union that we love our Creator, search for him, praise him, thank him, and take endless delight in him. And this is the plan that is at work continually in every single soul that is saved. This, as I have said before, is the divine will. And so in our creation, almighty God is the Father of our nature; and God, who is All-Wisdom, is the Mother of our nature together with the Love and Goodness of the Holy Ghost. This is all one God, one Lord. In this union, he is indeed our true husband and we his beloved wife, his fair maiden. He is never displeased with his wife, for he says, "I love you and you love me and love can never be broken."

I saw the activity of the whole blessed Trinity: in this vision I saw and understood these three attributes — Fatherhood, Motherhood, and Lordship — in one God. In our Father Almighty, we are sustained, made joyful, and redeemed as regards our essential nature from before the beginning of time. By the skill and wisdom of the Second Person, we are sustained, restored, and saved as regards our humanity, for he is our Mother, Brother, and Savior. And in our good Lord, the Holy Spirit, we have our reward and rest after our toil in this life, which exceeds anything we can desire — such is his wondrous courtesy and abundant grace.

For our life is also threefold. First, we have a Being; second, we have our development; and third, we have our fulfillment. The first stage is Nature, the second Mercy, and the third Grace.

First, I understood that the surpassing power of the Trinity is our Father and the profound Wisdom of the Trinity is our Mother, and the great Love of the Trinity is our Lord. We have received all this naturally, in our created and essential being.

Furthermore, I saw that the Second Person, who is our

Mother as regards our essential nature, has also become our Mother as regards our humanity. For God has created us twice: substance and humanity. Our essential nature is the higher part of ourselves, which we have in our Father. And the Second Person is the Mother of this essential nature, in the creation of our substance, in whom we are grounded and rooted. And he is also our Mother in his mercy because he has taken our humanity. Thus, our Mother describes the different ways in which he works, ways that are distinct from us but united in him. For in Christ our Mother, we grow and develop. In his mercy, he re-creates us and restores us and, by virtue of his Passion, death, and resurrection, he unites us to our own substance. This is the way our Mother mercifully works for all his children, who surrender to him and obey him.

But grace works with mercy, especially, as it was revealed, in two ways. This work belongs to the Third Person, the Holy Spirit. He works by rewarding and giving. Rewarding is the generous gift of truth, which the Lord gives to him who has made an effort. And giving is a courteous work that he gives freely by grace, perfect and exceeding any merits of his creatures.

So in our Father, God almighty, we have our being; in our merciful Mother, we have our re-creation and restoration by which our distinct parts are united and become a perfect man. In yielding to the Holy Spirit in grace we will be perfected.

And our essence is in our Father, God All-Mighty, and our substance is in our Mother, God All-Wise, and our substance is in our Lord the Holy Ghost, God All-Good. Our essence is complete in each person of the Trinity, which is one God. Our humanity is only in the Second Person, Christ Jesus. The Father and the Holy Ghost are in him too. In him and by him we have been powerfully taken out of hell, and out of the misery of the world, and carried up to heaven, blissfully united to our substance. And we have developed spiritual riches and honor through all Christ's virtues and the gracious activity of the Holy Spirit.

From Chapters 59–61: Jesus Is Our Mother

It is by means of mercy and grace that all this blessedness comes to us. We might never have possessed it or known it if the goodness that is God had not been opposed. That is why we have this happiness. Wickedness was allowed to rise up against the goodness, and the goodness of mercy and grace opposed the wickedness and transformed it all to goodness and honor for those who are going to be saved. For it is characteristic of God to pit goodness against evil. Thus, Jesus Christ, who does this, is our true Mother; we derive our being from him — and this is the foundation of Motherhood — together with all the sweet protection that follows this forever. For just as truly as God is our Father, so too God is our Mother. He has shown this in everything he has done, especially in the sweet words *It is I.* That is to say, *It is I, the Power and Goodness of the Fatherhood; it is I, the Wisdom of Motherhood; it is I, the Light and the grace that is blessed Love. I am the Sovereign Goodness of every single thing. It is I who makes you love, it is I who makes you yearn; it is I, the eternal fulfillment of every true desire.*

Jesus is the true Mother of our nature because he created us. He is also our Mother in grace, because he took our created nature. All the lovely activity and sweet business of beloved Motherhood is appropriated to the Second Person, for in him the godly will is completely safe forever, in nature and grace, because of his essential goodness. I understood that there were three ways of thinking about Motherhood in

God: the first is rooted in the fact that our nature is *created*; the second in the assumption of that human nature — and here is the origin of motherhood of grace. The third is that mother-hood of work, an outpouring by that same grace which flows over all things — the length, the breadth, the height, and the depths of it are eternal. And so is his love. . . .

Our Mother in nature and our Mother in grace — for he wanted to become our Mother in everything — humbly and gently laid the foundations of his work in the womb of the virgin. He showed me this in the first revelation, when he put into my mind an image of this humble virgin at the time of her conception. That is to say, in this lowly place, the supreme God, who is the sovereign wisdom, vested and arrayed him-self in our poor flesh. He himself was preparing to serve as a mother in all its aspects.

A mother's is the most intimate, most spontaneous, and most faithful work because it is the most genuine. No one else has been able to perform that office as perfectly as he — nor will they. We know that all our mothers bore us painfully, sometimes even dying in their labor, and look at what our true Mother Jesus, the all-love, has done! He has borne us to joy and to eternal life, blessed be he! He has carried us within himself lovingly; he has labored until the time came for him to suffer the sharpest pains and the most grievous agony that has ever been endured and, finally, he died. And when his work was over and he had introduced us into the eternal life, his wondrous love is still not satisfied. He revealed this in those exalted words: *If I could suffer more, I would.*

He could not die again, but he did not stop working. He needed to feed us next. His dear motherly love felt obliged to us. A mother suckles her child with milk, but our precious Mother Jesus feeds us with himself and he does it so courte-ously and tenderly with the Blessed Sacrament, the most precious food of life. Indeed, he sustains us mercifully and graciously with all the sweet sacraments, and that is what he meant by that blessed utterance: *It is I that Holy Church preaches and teaches*, which is as much as to say: *All the health and life of the sacraments, all the virtue and grace of my word, all the goodness which the Holy Church wants for you: it is I.* A mother holds her child tenderly to her breast, but our tender Mother Jesus takes us right inside his blessed breast, through his sweet open side, and there he shows us a glimpse of the Godhead and the joys of heaven. He revealed this in the tenth revelation, when he said, *Look! How I have loved you!* as he rejoiced while he gazed at his side.

This excellent and beloved word "Mother" is so sweet and natural in itself that it cannot really describe anyone but him and the woman who became his own mother and the mother of us all. Motherhood in itself implies a natural love, wisdom, and knowledge. And it is good; for even though our physical procreation is so insignificant and simple when it is compared to our spiritual regeneration, it is he who truly performs it in his creatures. A kind, loving mother who knows and understands what her child needs, looks after it very tenderly, as her maternal instinct requires. As the child grows older, she changes her methods, but not her love. When the child becomes older still, she allows it to be beaten to break it of its faults and help it to acquire virtue and grace. Our Lord does all these things and performs other offices that are fair and good. So it is he who is the mother of our nature, working through grace in the baser part of ourselves. And he wants us to realize this because he wants all our love to be directed to him. When I thought this over, I saw that everything we owe, by God's command, to our mothers and fathers, is brought to perfection in a true love of God. And it is Christ who activates this blessed love in our hearts. This was revealed throughout the revelations, especially in the rich and sublime words *It is I whom you love.*

After he has given birth to us spiritually, he looks after us with incredible tenderness, because he thinks that our souls are more valuable than our bodies. He kindles our understanding, guides our way, eases our conscience, comforts our soul, enlightens our heart, and gives us a glimpse of knowledge and faith in his blessed Godhead. When we remember his humanity and his passion we acquire a proper admiration of his surpassing goodness. He causes us to love what he loves for love of him and to be delighted by him and with all that he has done. When we fall, he hurries to pick us up, and gently comforts and fondles us. Strengthened by his activity within us, we are able to serve him voluntarily and love him with all our hearts, by grace, forever and ever.

But he allows some of us to have a more serious or dangerous fall — at least that is how it seems to us. And then, because we are not very clever, we imagine that this has canceled out all our achievements. But this is not true. For we needed to fall; we needed to watch ourselves falling. If we never fell we should never realize how feeble and wretched we are in ourselves nor know the wondrous love of our Creator. In heaven we shall see how grievously we have sinned during our earthly life for all eternity, and yet in spite of this we shall see that we never damaged his love for us nor did we become less precious to him. This fall means that we shall have a lofty and wonderful knowledge of God forever. For the kind of love that cannot and will not be broken by sin is extraordinarily strong. It is important to know this. Another good lesson we can learn when we watch ourselves fall is a humbling sense of our own unimportance and, as we know, this will help to raise us up to heaven — something that might never have happened without our humiliation. So we needed to see it, and if we don't gain in humility no fall will help us. Usually we fall first and only realize what has happened later — both through the mercy of God.

Sometimes a mother lets her child fall and get hurt to teach him a lesson, but because of her love for him, she will never expose her child to anything dangerous. An earthly mother can let her child die, but our heavenly Mother, Jesus, will never permit any one of his children to perish, for he is All-Mighty, All-Wise, and All-Love. Blessed be he!

But often when our failure and helplessness has been revealed to us, we are very frightened and so deeply ashamed that we don't know where to put ourselves. But our kindly mother doesn't want us to run away: in fact, there is nothing he wants less. But he wants us to behave like a child when it is hurt or frightened and rushes to its mother for help as fast as it can. He wants us to do this and say to him with the humility of a child, "My kind Mother, my gracious Mother, my beloved Mother, have mercy on me. I have got myself into a horrible mess and am not at all like you. Without your help and your grace, I cannot make things better." Even if we don't feel better immediately, we can be sure that he is treating us like a wise mother. If he sees that it is better for us to mourn and weep he lets us for as long as he thinks best, with pity and compassion and because he loves us. And here again he wants us to behave like a child who naturally trusts his mother's love implicitly.

He also wants us to hold staunchly to the faith of Holy Church and find our beloved Mother in that communion of saints. He gives us the comfort of complete understanding. An individual can be broken — or so it seems to him — but not the whole Body of Holy Church, which can never be destroyed and which is eternal. So it is a good and gracious idea, and one that brings us security to desire to be fastened and united to our Mother Holy Church, which is Christ Jesus. For his precious blood and water, which is food to many, flows copiously to make us fair and pure. The blessed wounds of our Savior are open and he takes pleasure in healing us; the sweet, gracious hands of our Mother are always open to help us. In all this, Jesus assumes the office of kind nurse who has no other business but to take care of the ultimate well-being of her child.

It is his duty to save us; it is glory to do it and he wants us to know this: he wants us to love him sweetly and put our trust in him strongly and with humility. He revealed this to me in these gracious words: *I keep you entirely safe.*

From Chapter 63: All Will Be Well

So our life depends on Jesus our true Mother, and has been rooted in him through his own providential Wisdom from before the beginning of time, with the exalted Power of the Father and the exalted and sovereign Goodness of the Holy Ghost. When he assumed our human nature, he gave life to us; in his blessed death on the Cross, he bore us into everlasting life and from that time to this and right up to the Day of Judgment, he feeds us and encourages us, as the supreme and sovereign Mother and as the natural needs of childhood demand.

How fair and sweet our heavenly Mother is in the eyes of our soul; how precious and lovely are those who have been made his children by grace in our heavenly Mother's eyes: they are gentle and humble, with all the attractive and natural traits of childhood; the natural child never despairs of its mother's love, never relies on itself, loves his mother and all the other children. These qualities, and others like them, are beautiful and they enable us to serve and please our Mother in heaven.

I also understood that childhood is the highest state of life here below because of weakness and helplessness of mind and body until our heavenly Mother brings us into the bliss of our Father. Then the true meaning of his sweet words will be revealed to us: *All will be well: and you yourself will see that every conceivable thing will be well.* And then the blessed Motherhood of Christ will begin a new phase in the joy of our God. It will be a new era, a new heaven and a new earth that will last forever.

And so I understand that all his children who have been blessedly born to him in nature will be brought to him again by grace.

Chapter 65: Salvation

And so I realized that a man or woman who deliberately chooses God in this life out of love for him can be sure that they themselves are loved extremely. This endless love is activated by grace within the soul, for God wants us to be confident in our hope for heaven during this life, and once we are there we shall be quite secure. The more pleasure and joy we have in this confidence, the better he likes it, as the revelations show, provided it is informed by a proper reverence and humility. The reverence I mean is a holy fear of our Lord that does not take him for granted and is linked to humility, whereby a creature sees the astonishing greatness of God and its own astonishing littleness. The people who are loved by God possess these virtues for all eternity. They can also be seen and experienced in this life too when the gracious presence of our Lord makes itself felt. We should yearn for this gracious presence of our Lord in all things more than anything else, because it produces a marvelous confidence in true faith and sure hope and a sweet, delightful fear because of his great charity.

It is God's will that I see myself to be as much beholden to him in love as if he had done everything just for me. This should be the interior attitude of every soul toward its Lover. The charity of God created such a unity that, when it is seen correctly, nobody can separate himself from anybody else. This is the way that our soul can think that God has done everything for it alone.

God revealed this to make us love him and fear only him. For he wants us to realize that the whole power of our enemy has been taken into the hands of our Friend; and therefore the soul that is confident of this will not be afraid of anyone but the One he loves. It ascribes any other fear to our emotions, to physical illness and fantasy. And therefore even if we are in so much pain, sorrow, and distress that we seem unable to think of anything but the trouble we are in, we should pass over it lightly as soon as we can and regard it as nothing. Why? Because it is God's will that we know him, and if we know him, love him, and fear him reverently, we will have peace and great rest and everything he does will please us. Our Lord revealed this to me when he said, *Why should it grieve you to suffer for a while, since it is my will and for my glory?*

I have now described fifteen revelations to you, as God deigned to put them into my mind and which I have renewed by later illuminations and, I hope, by the touch of the same Spirit who revealed them all originally. These fifteen revelations began early in the morning at about four o'clock and then proceeded in a steady, regular order, one after the other, until it was past nine.

Chapter 66: Julian Loses Faith in Her Revelations

Our Lord showed me the sixteenth revelation on the following night, as I shall relate: this sixteenth showing was the conclusion and confirmation of the previous fifteen.

But first I have to tell you how feeble, small-minded, and

blind I was. At the outset I had said, "And at that moment all
my pain was suddenly taken from me." I had no further pain,
grief, or distress as long as the fifteen revelations lasted. And
when my Lord had finished, everything closed down and I
saw no more. And I felt that I was going to live, but the next
moment my sickness returned: first in my head, with horrible
noises, and then my whole body was immediately invaded by
disease as before. And I felt as barren and desolate as if I had
had no comfort at all. And, wretched creature that I was, I
moaned and wept as I felt the pains of my body and the lack of
comfort physical and spiritual.

Then a religious person came and asked me how I was. I
said, "I was raving today." And he laughed, loudly and heart-
ily. And I said, "The crucifix that was put before my face
seemed to pour with blood." At that, the person I was speaking to sobered up and was amazed. And I then felt deeply
ashamed and astonished at my thoughtlessness, thinking,
"This man takes my least word quite seriously." So I said no
more about it. And when I saw that he took it seriously and
reverently, I wept, feeling very ashamed, and I wanted to go
to confession. But at the same time, I could not tell a priest all
this, for I thought: "Why should a priest believe me? I don't
even believe our Lord God." I really had believed at the time
that I had seen him and I had longed and intended to see him
soon in eternity but, like a fool, I had let the revelations slip
from my mind. Oh, what a poor creature I am! This was a
great sin and most ungrateful that because of a pathetic
amount of physical pain, I was stupid enough to lose for a
while all the comfort of the whole blessed revelation from our
Lord God. Here you can see what sort of person I am when
left to myself!

But our courteous Lord would not leave me in this state. I
lay quietly until nightfall, trusting in his mercy, and then I fell
asleep. And in my first sleep it seemed to me that the Fiend had

me by the throat, putting his face close to mine. He had a face like a young man's, long and extraordinarily thin: I never saw anything like it. It was as red as a newly baked tile, but was dirtier than tiling because it was covered with black spots like freckles. He had rusty red hair, short in front with long locks dangling from his temples. He grinned at me maliciously, showing white teeth that made it, I thought, even more horrible. His body and hands were misshapen, but with his paws he held me by the throat and tried to strangle me but could not.

This horrible revelation came in my sleep, unlike all the others. But throughout it I still trusted that I would be preserved through God's mercy. And our courteous Lord allowed me to wake up. I was barely alive. The people who were with me saw and bathed my temples and my heart began to revive. And then a little smoke came through the door with great heat and a foul stench. *Benedicite Domine!* I said. "The house is on fire!" I thought it was a real fire that would burn us all to death. But they said no, they saw nothing there. "Blessed be God!" I said, for I knew then that it had been the Fiend who had come to molest me. And immediately I remembered what our Lord had shown me that very day, together with the faith of Holy Church — for the two were the same — and I flew to this for comfort. Then it all vanished and I was brought to great rest and peace, with no sickness of body and no fears of conscience.

Chapter 67: The Sixteenth Revelation

And our Lord opened my inner eye and showed me my soul in the middle of my heart. The soul was as large as an infinite world and like a blessed kingdom. From what I saw there, I understood that it is a glorious City. In the midst of it sits our Lord Jesus, God and man, splendid, powerfully built,

highest bishop, most majestic king, most worshipful Lord. I saw him in his majestic regalia. And he sits in glory within the soul, his proper abode of peace and rest. The Godhead rules and preserves heaven and earth and all that is — sovereign Power, sovereign Wisdom, and sovereign Goodness. Jesus will never leave the place that he has occupied in our soul forever and ever, I think. For in us he is entirely at home and has an everlasting dwelling.

And in this revelation, he showed me the satisfaction he takes in the creation of a man's soul. For a man's soul was made as well as Father, Son, and Holy Ghost could make a creature. And so it was done. And therefore the Trinity takes an endless pleasure in the creation of man's soul, for he saw that it would please him forever from before the beginning of time.

From Chapter 81: God in the Soul

Our good Lord revealed himself to me in various *ways* in heaven and earth, but the only *place* I saw him dwelling was in the soul of man.

He revealed himself on earth in the sweet incarnation and in his blessed Passion. He showed himself on earth in another way, when I said, "I saw God in a point." And in yet another way he revealed himself on earth as though he were on a pilgrimage, or, in other words, he is here with us, guiding us, and he will remain with us until he has led us all to the bliss of heaven. As I have said before, he revealed himself reigning in glory in various ways, but chiefly in the soul of man. There he has set up his resting place and his glorious City and from this honored dwelling he will never rise to depart forever and ever.

From Chapter 82: God's View of Sin

But here our courteous Lord showed me the soul groaning and grief-stricken and explained, *I know perfectly well that you want to live and love me and to suffer joyfully and gladly all the penance that comes to you. But because you do not live without sin, you want to endure, for love of me, all the sorrow, tribulation, and distress that comes your way. And this is right. But don't be too disturbed by the sins that you commit involuntarily.*

Here I understood that our Lord looks upon his servant with pity, not with blame. For this transitory life of ours does not require us to live entirely free from either blame or sin. God loves us eternally, and yet we are always sinning! He shows us this gently and then we are sorry and mourn over each sin. We turn to gaze at his mercy, clinging to his love and goodness, realizing that he is our medicine and that we do nothing but sin. So from the humility we acquire from this vision of our sinfulness, yet knowing and putting our trust in his endless love, we thank him, praise him, and please him: *I love you and you love me and our love shall never be broken: it was for your benefit that I suffer these things.* All this was revealed to the understanding of my soul with these blessed words: *I keep you entirely safe.*

And through the great desire in our blessed Lord that we should live in this way, that is, in longing and joy, this lesson of love shows, I came to understand, that not all our disadvantages come from God but from the Enemy. He wants us to know this, by the gracious, sweet light of his compassionate love. If there is any person on the face of the earth who loves God but never commits a sin, I don't know anything about it! It wasn't revealed to me.

But this *was* revealed: that when we fall and when we rise we are still preserved in exactly the same Love. In God's eyes we do not fall: in our own eyes we never stand upright! Both these visions are true, I think. But the viewpoint of God is the higher truth.

Chapter 86: Love Was His Meaning

This book was begun by the gift and grace of God and, in my view, it isn't finished yet.

We all pray for charity. God is at work in us, making us thankful, trustful, and joyful. This is how our Lord wants us to pray to him, as I understood his intentions in the sweet words, which he said so cheerfully, *I am the ground of your prayer.* I realized that the reason our Lord had revealed this was because he wants it to be better known than it is. When we know this, he will give us the grace to love him and cling to him. For he looks upon his heavenly treasure here on earth with such great love that he wants to give us even more light and consolation in the joys of heaven. And so he draws our hearts toward him, away from the sorrow and darkness in which we live.

From the time that this was originally revealed to me, I often wanted to learn what our Lord had meant by it. And more than fifteen years later, I received this spiritual illumination when he said, *Do you want to see your Lord's meaning? Learn it well: Love was his meaning. Who showed it to you? Love. Why did he show it to you? For love. Hold fast to this and you will learn and understand more and more. But you will never learn or know anything else throughout eternity.* This taught me that love was our Lord's meaning.

And I saw with absolute certainty that before God made us, he loved us. This love has never faltered and it never will. In this love he has done all his works and he has made everything work out for our good. In this love we will live forever. We began when we were created, but the love in which he created us had no beginning. Our beginning is in this love, and we shall see all this in God forever and ever.

Amen, Jesus, Amen.

Notes

I. *The Fire of Love*

1. *Legenda,* Lesson 1. Quoted and translated in F. M. Comper, *The Life and Lyrics of Richard Rolle*, London, 1928, p. 302.
2. I Corinthians 13:12.
3. Paraphrase from Exodus 20:6.
4. James 1:5.
5. Job 19:18.
6. Galatians 2:20.
7. Song of Solomon 5:8.
8. I Corinthians 2:15.
9. Psalm 109:28.
10. Ecclesiasticus 1:14.
11. Psalm 42:2.
12. Galatians 5:17.
13. Matthew 20:15.
14. Ecclesiasticus 10:1.
15. II Corinthians 12:2.

II. *The Cloud of Unknowing*

1. Exodus 19:9–25.
2. Luke 10:38–42 in the Jerusalem Bible translation.
3. Matthew 17:1–8; Mark 9:2–8; Luke 9:28–36.

III. *The Ladder of Perfection*

1. Romans 12:2.
2. *Commentaries on the Sentences,* 1.2.
3. *Soliloquies,* 1.7.
4. *The Ascent of Mount Carmel,* 2:2.
5. Ephesians 3:17–18. In this as in later passages, Hilton does not give a literal translation of the Latin but a rough paraphrase that inserts his own ideas and words into the text.
6. Matthew 5:8.
7. Job 5:26.
8. Psalm 142:1.
9. Psalm 69:1.
10. Psalm 41:4.
11. Psalm 136:1.
12. I Corinthians 14:14–15.
13. Leviticus 6:12.
14. Luke 10:27.
15. Acts of the Apostles 2:4, 11.
16. Psalm 51:1.
17. I Corinthians 2:2.
18. Galatians 6:14.
19. I Corinthians 1:24.
20. Luke 13:24.
21. Matthew 16:24.

22. Colossians 3:5.
23. Psalm 49:20.
24. Luke 10:42.
25. Deuteronomy 11:24.
26. Luke 15:8–9.
27. Psalm 119:105.
28. Matthew 6:22.
29. Matthew 5:15.
30. Psalm 19:12.
31. John 14:21.
32. Matthew 11:29.
33. John 13:34–5.
34. Romans 8:1.
35. I John 2:10.
36. Micah 7:8.
37. Colossians 3:3.
38. Matthew 19:29.
39. Psalm 73:22.
40. Isaiah 50:10.
41. Isaiah 58:10, 11.
42. Isaiah 47:5.
43. Romans 12:2.
44. Colossians 1:9.
45. Ephesians 4:23–4.
46. Colossians 3:9–10.
47. I John 3:2.
48. I John 4:8.
49. I John 4:19.

IV. *Revelations of Divine Love*

1. *Spiritual Relations,* 6.
2. These "wounds," of course, are not physical. As Julian goes on to explain, they are spiritual sufferings that will bring her close to God.

Selected Bibliography

I have used the following edited texts:

Deanesly, Margaret (ed.), *The Incendium Amoris of Richard Rolle of Hampole,* Manchester

Guy, E., *The Scale of Perfection,* London, 1869.

Hodgson, Phyllis, *The Cloud of Unknowing,* E.E.T.S., Oxford, 1958.

Additional sources:

Arberry, A. J. *Sufism: An Account of the Mystics of Islam,* London, 1950.

Armstrong, Karen. *A Western Attempt to Understand Islam,* London.

————. *Tongues of Fire,* London, 1984.

Butler, Cuthbert. *Western Mysticism,* London, 1958.

Eliade, Mircea (trans. Wellard R. Trask), *The Sacred and the Profane, the Nature of Religion,* New York, 1959.

Green, Arthur (ed.), *Jewish Spirituality,* 2 Vols., London, 1986 and 1988.

Heschel, Abraham J., *The Prophets,* 2 Vols., New York, 1962.

Inge, W. R., *Christian Mysticism*, London, 1899.

———. *Studies of the English Mystics*, London 1906.

Katz, Teven T. (ed.), *Mysticism and Religious Tradition*, Oxford, 1983.

Kirk, K. E., *The Vision of God*, London, 1931.

Knowles, Dom David, *The English Mystics*, London, 1927.

Leclercq, J. (ed.), *Spirituality of the Middle Ages*, London, 1968.

Lings, Martin, *Muhammad, His Life Based on the Earliest Sources*, London, 1983.

Lossky, Vladimir, *The Mystical Theology of the Eastern Church*, London, 1957.

McGinn, Bernard and John Meyendorff, (eds.), *Christian Spirituality: Origins to the Twelfth Century*, London, 1985.

McGrath, Alister E., *Reformation Thought, An Introduction*, Oxford and New York, 1988.

Meyendorff, John, *Byzantine Theology, Historical Trends and Doctrinal Themes*, New York and London, 1975.

Nasr, Seyyed Hossein (ed.), *Islamic Spirituality: Foundation*, London, 1987.

Nicholson, R. A., *The Mystics of Islam*, London, 1914.

Pepler, C., *The English Religious Heritage*, London, 1958.

Rolt, C. E., *Dionysius the Areopagite*, London, 1920.

Scholem, Gershom G., *Major Trends in Jewish Mysticism*, 2nd. Ed., London, 1955.

Sitwell, G., *Medieval Spiritual Writers*, London, 1961.

Thornton, M., *English Spirituality*, London, 1963.

Underhill, Evelyn, *The Mystics of the Church*, London, 1933.

Walsh, John, *Pre-Reformation English Spirituality*, London, 1965.

Woods, Richard (ed.), *Understanding Mysticism*, London and New York, 1980.

About the Author

KAREN ARMSTRONG entered a Roman Catholic order of nuns at the age of seventeen, taking vows of poverty, chastity, and obedience in 1965. During her years as a nun she studied theology, Scripture, and church history, and in 1967 the order sent her to Oxford University to read English. In 1969, she decided to write a thesis on Tennyson. She left Oxford to teach, first at Bedford College, University of London, and then at James Allen's Girls' School in Dulwich.

In 1982, Karen Armstrong became a broadcaster and freelance writer. She is the author of two volumes of autobiography about her life as a nun, *Through the Narrow Gate* and *Beginning the World*. In 1984 her documentary, "The First Christian," was shown on television and published in book form. Other television series have included *Varieties of Religious Experience* and *Tongues of Fire*. She is the author of *The Gospel According to Women* and *Holy War*, and the recent bestseller *The History of God*.

Karen Armstrong lives in North London.